Simplified Living Will Kit

by Daniel Sitarz
Attorney-at-Law

Nova Publishing Company
Small Business and Consumer Legal Books and Software
Carbondale, Illinois

ISBN 1-892949-22-9   Book ($15.95)

Cataloging-in-Publication Data
    Sitarz, Dan, 1948-
        Simplified Living Will Kit / by Daniel Sitarz. -- 1st ed.--Carbondale, ILL.:
          Nova Publishing Company, 2005
        128 p. cm. -- (National Legal Kit series).
        1. Forms (Law)—United States—Popular Works. 2. Civil Law—United States—Forms.
        I. Sitarz, Daniel. II. Title. III. Series.
        ISBN 1-892949-22-9   Book ($15.95)

Nova Publishing Company is dedicated to providing up-to-date and accurate legal information to the public. All Nova publications are periodically revised to contain the latest available legal information.

1st Edition; 1st Printing   January, 2006

This publication is designed to provide accurate and authoritative information in regard to the subject matter covered. It is sold with the understanding that the publisher and author are not engaged in rendering legal, accounting, or other professional services. If legal advice or other expert assistance is required, the services of a competent professional person should be sought.

—From a Declaration of Principles jointly adopted by a Committee of the American Bar Association and a Committee of Publishers

DISCLAIMER

Because of possible unanticipated changes in governing statutes and case law relating to the application of any information contained in this book, the author, publisher, and any and all persons or entities involved in any way in the preparation, publication, sale, or distribution of this book disclaim all responsibility for the legal effects or consequences of any document prepared or action taken in reliance upon information contained in this book. No representations, either express or implied, are made or given regarding the legal consequences of the use of any information contained in this book. Purchasers and persons intending to use this book for the preparation of any legal documents are advised to check specifically on the current applicable laws in any jurisdiction in which they intend the documents to be effective.

Nova Publishing Company
Small Business and Consumer Legal Books and Software
1103 West College Street
Carbondale, IL 62901
Editorial: (800) 748-1175

Distributed by:
National Book Network
4501 Forbes Blvd., Suite 200
Lanham, MD 20706
Orders: (800) 462-6420

Nova Publishing Company Green Business Policies

Nova Publishing Company is committed to preserving ancient forests and natural resources. Our company's policy is to print all of our books on recycled paper, with no less than 30% post-consumer waste de-inked in a chlorine-free process. In addition, all Nova books are printed using soy-based inks. As a result, for the printing of this book, we have saved:

7.26 trees • 2,100 gallons of water • 1,230 kilowatt hours of electricity • 18 pounds of pollution

Nova Publishing Company is a member of Green Press Initiative, a nonprofit program dedicated to supporting publishers in their efforts to reduce their use of fiber obtained from endangered forests. For more information, go to www.greenpressinitiative.org. In addition, Nova uses all compact fluorescent lighting; recycles all office paper products, aluminum and plastic beverage containers, and printer cartridges; uses 100% post-consumer fiber, process-chlorine-free, acid-free paper for 95% of in-house paper use; and, when possible, uses electronic equipment that is EPA Energy Star-certified. Finally, all carbon emissions from office energy use are offset by the purchase of wind-energy credits that are used to subsidize the building of wind turbines on the Rosebud Sioux Reservation in South Dakota (see www.nativeenergy.com/coop).

Table of Contents

Planning Your Health Care Options

What is a Living Will?

A living will is a relatively new legal document that has been made necessary due to recent technological advances in the field of medicine. These advances can allow for the continued existence of a person on advanced life support systems long after any normal semblance of "life," as many people consider it, has ceased. The inherent problem that is raised by this type of extraordinary medical "life support" is that the person whose life is being artificially continued by such means may not wish to be kept alive beyond what they may consider to be the proper time for their life to end. However, since a person in such condition has no method of communicating their wishes to the medical or legal authorities in charge, a living will was developed that allows one to make these important decisions in advance of the situation. The purpose of a living will is to provide doctors and other health care workers with clear directions regarding how you would like your medical care handled toward the end of your life. A living will makes it possible for you to specify, in advance, exactly what your preferences are regarding the use of life-sustaining medical procedures if you are ever in a terminal medical condition or in a vegetative state, and are unable to give such directions yourself. *Terminal* is generally defined as an incurable condition that will cause imminent death such that the use of life-sustaining procedures only serve to prolong the moment of death. Likewise, a *vegetative state* is generally defined as a complete and irreversible loss of cognitive brain function and consciousness. Thus, a living will comes into effect only when there is no medical hope for a recovery from a particular injury or illness which will prove fatal or leave one in a permanent and irreversible coma.

As more and more advances are made in the medical field in terms of the ability to prevent "clinical" death, the difficult situations envisioned by a living will are destined to occur more often. Although a living will does not address all possible contingencies regarding terminally-ill patients, it does provide a written declaration for the individual to make known her or his decisions on life-prolonging procedures. A living will declares your wishes not to be kept alive by artificial or mechanical means if you are suffering from a terminal condition and your death would be imminent without the use of such artificial means. It provides a legally-binding written set of instructions regarding your wishes about this important matter. In most states, in order to qualify for the use of a living will, you must meet the following criteria:

- You must be at least 18 years of age
- You must be of "sound mind"
- You must be able to comprehend the nature of your action in signing such a document

A living will becomes valid when it has been properly signed and witnessed. However, it is very important to remember that as long as you are capable of making decisions and giving directions regarding your medical care, your stated wishes must be followed–not those directions that are contained in your living will. Your living will only comes into force when you are in a terminal or vegetative condition, with no likelihood of recovery, and are unable to provide directions yourself. Until that time, you–and not your living will–will provide the directions for your health care. Generally, a licensed physician is required to determine when your condition has become terminal or vegetative with no likelihood of recovering.

The forms contained in this kit are taken directly from the most recent legislation regarding living wills in each state. A few states do not currently have specific legislation providing express statutory recognition of living wills. For those states, a living will has been prepared by legal professionals to comply with the basic requirements that courts in that state or other states have found important. In such states, be assured that courts, health care professionals, and physicians will be guided by this expression of your desires concerning life support as expressed in the living will prepared using this kit. Please select the appropriate form for use in your own state.

Typical Living Wills Provisions

Nearly all states have passed legislation setting up a statutorily-accepted living will form. Those states that have not expressed a preference for a specific type of living will have, nevertheless, accepted living wills that adhere to general legal requirements. There are many different types of living wills, from very brief statements such as the following from the state of Illinois:

> "If at any time I should have an incurable and irreversible injury, disease, or illness judged to be a terminal condition by my attending physician who has personally examined me and has determined that my death is imminent except for death-delaying procedures, I direct that such procedures which would only prolong the dying process be withheld or withdrawn, and that I be permitted to die naturally with only the administration of medication, sustenance, or the performance of any medical procedure deemed necessary by my attending physician to provide me with comfort care."

to lengthy and elaborate multi-page forms with detailed and very specific instructions. All of the various state forms try to assure that a person's own wishes are followed regarding health care decisions. Many states have drafted their legislation with the intention that people prepare both a living will and a Health Care Power of Attorney (or similar form) which appoints a person of your choosing to act on your behalf in making health care decisions when you are unable to make such decisions for yourself. It is advisable to prepare both of these forms in order to cover most, if not all, eventualities that may arise regarding your health care in difficult situations. In general, the purpose of your living will is to convey your wishes regarding life-prolonging treatment and artificially provided nutrition and hydration if you no longer have the capacity to make your own decisions, have a terminal condition, or become permanently unconscious, in particular the following two situations:

- Whether treatment be withheld or withdrawn, and that you be permitted to die naturally with only the administration of medication or the performance of any medical treatment deemed necessary to alleviate pain. This would generally mean the withdrawal of assistance with breathing, withdrawal of artificial maintenance of blood pressure and heart rate, withdrawal of kidney dialysis, and the cessation of other similar procedures.

- Whether you desire the withholding or withdrawal of artificially-provided food, water, or other artificially provided nourishment or fluids.

Living wills generally provide, in the absence of your own ability to give directions regarding the use of life-prolonging treatment and artificially-provided nutrition and hydration, that it is your intention that your living will be honored by your attending physician, family, and anyone else as the final expression of your legal right to refuse medical or surgical treatment. Most forms also state that by signing the form you fully accept the consequences of the refusal of medical care in the circumstances that you have chosen. In addition, in many states, if you have been diagnosed as pregnant and that diagnosis is known to your attending physician, your living will has no legal force or effect during the course of your pregnancy.

There may be situations in which the use of a living will is not appropriate. For example, the official living will forms in some states may actually forbid a doctor from withdrawing all life support in terminal situations. These forms may forbid the withdrawal of "nutrition and hydration," essentially tube-type feeding for terminally ill patients. You will need to review the precise terms of the living will form for your state to be certain that it is what you want. You may desire to complete and sign a Health Care Power of Attorney and Appointment of Health Care Agent to complete your advance health care options.

Witness Requirements

All states which have enacted legislation regarding living wills or their counterparts have provided protections to ensure the validity of the living will. They have also provided legal protections against persons using undue influence to force or coerce someone into signing a living will. There are various requirements regarding who may be a witness to your signing of your living will. In general, these protections are for the purpose of ensuring that the witnesses have no actual or indirect stake in your death. These witnesses should have no connection with you from a health care or beneficiary standpoint. In most states, the witnesses must:

- Be at least 18 years of age
- Not be related to you in any manner: by blood, marriage, or adoption
- Not be your attending physician
- Not be a patient or employee of your attending physician
- Not be a patient, physician, or employee of the health care facility in which you may be a patient
- Not be entitled to any portion of your estate upon your death under any laws of intestate succession, nor under your will or any codicil
- Have no claim against any portion of your estate upon your death
- Not be directly financially responsible for your medical care
- Not have signed the living will for you, even at your direction
- Not be paid a fee for acting as a witness

These restrictions on who may be a witness to your signing of a living will require, in most cases, that the witnesses be either friends who will receive nothing from you under your will, or strangers. Please review the requirements for your own state in the Appendix of this book.

In addition, please note that several states and the District of Columbia have laws in effect regarding witnesses when the *declarant* (the legal term for the person signing a living will–someone who is making a declaration regarding his or her health care choices) is a patient in a nursing home, boarding facility, hospital, or skilled or intermediate health care facility. In those situations, it is advisable to have a patient ombudsman, patient advocate, or the director of the health care facility to act as the third witness to the signing of a living will. Also note that some states provide a choice as to the method by which your living will is witnessed: you may choose to have two (2) witnesses sign your living will or you may choose to have it notarized by a notary public. Please check the specific witness requirements that are shown on the living will form for your state.

Health Care Power of Attorney and Appointment of Health Care Agent:

This legal document may also be referred to as a Durable Health Care Power of Attorney, or Appointment of a Health Care Proxy, or some similar title. This document goes beyond the provisions of a living will and provides for health care options that living wills do not cover. It is an important addition to the use of a living will. Basically, a Health Care Power of Attorney and Appointment of Health Care Agent is used to appoint someone to act for you in making health care decisions when you are unable to make them for yourself. A living will does not provide for this. In addition, a Health Care Power of Attorney and Appointment of Health Care Agent generally applies to all medical decisions (unless you specifically limit the power). Most living wills only apply to certain decisions regarding life support at the end of your life. Living wills are, thus, most useful in terminal illness and/or permanent coma situations. Finally, a Health Care Power of Attorney and Appointment of Health Care Agent can provide specific detailed instructions regarding what you would like done by your attending physician in specific circumstances. Generally, living wills are limited instructions regarding providing or withholding of life support options.

A Health Care Power of Attorney and Appointment of Health Care Agent form is provided in this kit. Many states have enacted legislation regarding this type of form and all states recognize the validity of this type of legal document. Information regarding each states' provisions are included in the Appendix. In order to be certain that you have made provisions for most potential health care situations, it is recommended that you prepare both a living will and a Health Care Power of Attorney and Appointment of Health Care Agent.

Obviously, your choice of a person to act as your *health care agent* (the person you appoint with your Health Care Power of Attorney and Appointment of Health Care Agent) will need to be someone that you trust fully. You will be placing life and death decision-making power in his or her hands. In many cases, a spouse is the natural choice for selection as your health care agent. A son or daughter may also be a wise choice in some situations. In any case, the decision regarding whom you select as your health care agent is yours personally and it may, literally, be a life-or-death decision. If you feel pressured or coerced into signing such a powerful document as a living will or Health Care Power of Attorney and Appointment of Health Care Agent, you should immediately get legal assistance or notify your doctor and request help.

There may also arise a situation in which the terms of your living will conflict with the decisions of the person whom you have named as your health care agent. The laws in most states, and indeed, most physicians will honor the decisions of your health care agent to provide medical care to keep you alive, even if it conflicts with your specific desires to withhold medical care, as stated in your living will. Keep this in mind as you discuss the appointment of someone as your health care agent. If you want your health care agent to adhere to the terms of your living will in all cases, you should make that important point clear to your health care agent.

Organ Donation Form

The use of this type of form allows you to make a donation of your organs. Using this form youmake choices about whether and how you may wish any of your organs to be donated for medical, scientific, or educational uses after your death. All states have versions of a state law (usually referred to as an "Anatomical Gift Act") that provides that individuals may make personal choices about whether and how to provide the gift of their organs after death. Because of the many lives that can be saved through the use of transplanted donated organs, many states actively encourage such donations. Although the use of this form is voluntary, its use can save the lives of some of the many people who are in desperate need of donated organs. You may choose to either donate all of your organs or limit your donation to specific organs. Likewise, you may provide that your organs be used for any purpose or you may limit their use to certain purposes. Please read through the form carefully, make your appropriate decisions and sign the form in front of two witness, who should also sign the form.

Preparing and Signing Your Living Will and Other Forms

Select the appropriate form or forms for your state from the included forms. Carefully read through the entire living will for your state and, if desired, the Health Care Power of Attorney and Appointment of Health Care Agent and Organ Donation Form that are provided. Make the appropriate choices in each form where indicated. Be careful so that you are certain that you are expressing your desires exactly how you wish on this very important matter. When you have a completed original, staple all of the pages together in the upper left-hand corner. ***Do not yet sign this document or fill in the date.***

You should now assemble your witnesses and/or a Notary Public to witness your signature. As noted in the Appendix, be certain that your witnesses meet your specific state requirements. In addition, please note that several states and the District of Columbia have laws in effect regarding witnesses when the declarant is a patient in a nursing home, boarding facility, hospital, or skilled or intermediate health care facility. In those situations, it is advisable to have a patient ombudsman, patient advocate, or the director of the health care facility to act as the third witness to the signing of a living will.

There is no requirement that the witnesses know any of the terms of your living will or other documents or that they read any of your living will. All that is necessary is that they observe you sign your living will and other documents and that they also sign the documents as witnesses in each others' presence.

In front of all of the witnesses and/or the Notary Public, the following should take place in the order shown:

① You will sign your living will and each of the other documents selected at the end of each document where indicated, exactly as your name is written on your living will, in ink using a pen.

② After you have signed, pass your living will and other documents to the first witness, who should sign where indicated and fill in her or his address, if required.

③ After the first witness has signed, have the living will and other documents passed to the second witness, who should also sign where indicated. Throughout this ceremony, you and all of the witnesses must remain together.

④ The final step, if required in your state, is for the Notary Public to sign in the space or spaces where indicated. When this step is completed, your living will and the other documents that you have signed are valid legal documents. Have several copies made and, if appropriate, deliver a copy to your attending physician to have placed in your medical records file. You may also desire to give a copy to your clergy and a copy to your spouse or other trusted relative.

Revocation of Living Will

All states that have recognized living wills have also provided easy methods revoke them. Since living wills provide authority to medical personnel to withhold life-support technology that will likely result in death to the patient, great care must be taken to insure that a change of mind by the patient is heeded. If revocation of your living will is an important issue, please consult your state's laws directly. For the revocation of a living will, any one of the following methods of revocation is generally acceptable:

• Physical destruction of the living will, such as tearing, burning, or mutilating the original of the document

• A written revocation of the living will by you or by a person acting at your direction. A form for this is provided. You may use two witnesses on this form, although most states do not require the use of witnesses for the written revocation of a living will to be valid.

• An oral revocation in the presence of a witness who signs and dates a writing confirming a revocation. This oral declaration may take any manner. Most states allow for a person to revoke such a document by any indication (even non-verbal) of the intent to revoke a living will, regardless of their physical or mental condition.

A blank Revocation of Living Will is provided in this kit. To complete this form, simply fill in the appropriate information and sign it in front of your witnesses. In addition, your two witnesses may sign it at the same time.

Revocation of Health Care Power of Attorney and Appointment of Health Care Agent

On the following page, there is included a Revocation of Health Care Power of Attorney. You have the right at any time to revoke your Health Care Power of Attorney. Remember, however, that should you become disabled or incapacitated and unable to communicate your wishes to anyone, you may be unable to communicate your desire to revoke your Health Care Power of Attorney. In any event, if you choose to revoke your health care power of attorney, a copy of this revocation should be provided to the person to whom the power was originally given. Copies should also be given to any party that may have had dealings with the attorney-in-fact before the revocation and to any party with whom the attorney-in-fact may be expected to attempt to deal with after the revocation, for example, your family physician.

This form should be filled out and signed by the person revoking the Health Care Power of Attorney. It should also be notarized.

Appendix: State Laws Regarding Living Wills

This Appendix contains a summary of the laws relating to living wills for all states and the District of Columbia (Washington D.C.). The state-by-state listings in this Appendix contain the following information for each state:

State Website: This listing provides the internet website address of the location of the state's statutes. The addresses were current at the time of this book's publication;, but website addresses are, or course, subject to change at any time.

State Law Description: This is the title where most of the relevant state laws on living wills are contained.

Living Will Form: Under this listing, the exact location of a state's official living will form is provided.

Other Directives: The existence and location of additional official state directives relating to advance health care and powers of attorney are indicated in this listing.

Living Will Effective: This listing indicates the requirements of state law regarding when a living will becomes effective.

Living Will Witness Requirements: Under this listing are noted the specific state requirements for witnesses to the signing of a living will and any related advance health care directives.

Alabama
State Website: www.legislature.state.al.us/CodeofAlabama/1975/coatoc.htm
State Law Reference: Code of Alabama.
Living Will Form: Living Will (Section 22-8A-4).
Other Directives: Durable Power of Attorney Act (Section 2612). Anatomical Gift Act (Section 22-19-40).
Living Will Effective: Two (2) physicians, one being the attending physician, must diagnose and document in the medical records that you either have a terminal illness or injury or are in a permanent state of unconsciousness.
Witness Requirements: Will must be signed in the presence of two (2) or more witnesses at least nineteen (19) years of age. Witnesses cannot be related by blood, adoption, or marriage, entitled to any part of your estate, or be directly financially responsible for your health care.

Alaska
State Website: www.legis.state.ak.us/folhome.htm
State Law Reference: Alaska Statutes.
Living Will Form: Declaration Relating to Use of Life Sustaining Procedures serves as Living Will (Section 18.12.010).
Other Directives: Durable Power of Attorney for Health Care (Section13.26.338 to 13.26.353). Anatomical Gift Act (Section 13.50.010 through 13.50.090). Durable Power of Attorney (Section 13.26.332).
Living Will Effective: Two (2) physicians determine that you are in a terminal condition and your death will result without using life sustaining procedures. Your physician must then record your diagnosis and the contents of your Declaration in your medical records.
Witness Requirements: Sign your Declaration, or direct another to sign it, in the presence of two (2) adult witnesses or a notary public. Witnesses cannot be related by blood or marriage.

Arizona
State Website: www.azleg.state.az.us/
State Law Reference: Arizona Revised Statutes Annotated.
Living Will Form: Living Will (Sections 36-3261 and 363262).
Other Directives: Health Care Power of Attorney (Section 363224). Anatomical Gift Act (Sections 36-841 through 36-850). Durable Power of Attorney (Section 14-5501).
Living Will Effective: For the living will to become operative, a physician must certify that your condition is terminal, irreversible, or incurable.
Witness Requirements: Sign in the presence of two (2) or more witnesses or a notary public. Witnesses cannot be related by blood, adoption, or marriage, entitled to any part of your estate, or be directly financially responsible for your health care.

Arkansas
State Website: http://www.arkleg.state.ar.us/
State Law Reference: Arkansas Code.
Living Will Form: Declaration serves as Living Will (Section 20-17-202).
Other Directives: Durable Power of Attorney for Health Care (Section 2013104). Anatomical Gift Act (Section 20-17-601). Durable Power of Attorney (Section 26-68-402).
Living Will Effective: Declaration applies when two (2) physicians diagnose you to have an incurable or irreversible condition that will cause death in a relatively short time.
Witness Requirements: Sign in the presence of two (2) witnesses. No other restrictions apply.

California
State Website: www.leginfo.ca.gov/
State Law Reference: California Law.
Living Will Form: California Advanced Health Care Directive serves as Living Will (Probate Code Section 4701)
Other Directives: California Advanced Health Care Directive contains Power of Attorney for Health Care, Instructions for Health Care, Donation of Organs, and Appointment of Primary Physician (Probate Code Section 4701). Anatomical Gift Act (Health and Safety Code Sections 7150 - 7158). Durable Power of Attorney (Probate Code Sections 4120 - 4230).
Living Will Effective: This Directive becomes effective in the event that you have an incurable and irreversible condition that will result in death within a relatively short time, become unconscious and, to a reasonable degree of medical certainty, will not regain consciousness, or the likely risks and burdens of treatment would outweigh the expected benefits.
Witness Requirements: Sign in the presence of two (2) adult witnesses. A witness cannot be the person you appointed as your agent, your health care provider or an employee of your health care provider, or the operator or employee of a residential care facility for the elderly. Witnesses cannot be related to you by blood, marriage, or adoption, or be entitled to any part of your estate. A third witness, who must be a patient advocate or ombudsman, is required if the patient is in a skilled nursing facility (Probate Code Section 4701).

Colorado
State Website: www.leg.state.co.us/
State Law Reference: Colorado Revised Statutes.
Living Will Form: Colorado Declaration as to Medical or Surgical Treatment serves as Living Will (Section 15-18-103).
Other Directives: Durable Power of Attorney for Health Care (Section 1514506). Anatomical Gift Act (Section 12-34-101). Durable Power of Attorney (Sections 15-1-1301 - 15-1-1320, 15-14-501 - 15-14-509 and 15-14-601 - 15-14-611).
Living Will Effective: Two (2) physicians must determine that you are in a terminal condition and your death will result without using life sustaining procedures. Your physician must then record your diagnosis and the contents of your Declaration in your medical records.

Witness Requirements: Sign in the presence of two (2) adult witnesses. A witness cannot be a person who has claim against your estate upon your death, stands to inherit from your estate, or a physician, an employee of your attending physician or treating health care facility, or a patient of your treating health care facility.

Connecticut

State Website: www.cga.state.ct.us/2001/pub/Titles.htm
State Law Reference: Connecticut General Statutes Annotated.
Living Will Form: Connecticut Health Care Instructions serves as Living Will (Section 19a-575).
Other Directives: Connecticut Health Care Instructions also contain Appointment of Health Care Agent and Appointment of Attorney In Fact for Health Care Decisions. Anatomical Gift Act (Section 19a-270). Durable Power of Attorney (Section 45a-562).
Living Will Effective: When you have an incurable or irreversible medical condition which, without the use of life support, will result in death in a relatively short period of time, or you are in a permanent coma or a persistent vegetative state.
Witness Requirements: Sign in the presence of two (2) adult witnesses. Your appointed agent cannot be a witness. If you reside in a resident facility operated or licensed by the department of mental health or department of mental retardation, additional witness requirements must be met and you should consult an attorney.

Delaware

State Website: www.delcode.state.de.us/
State Law Reference: Delaware Code Annotated.
Living Will Form: Instructions for Health Care serves as Living Will (Section 16-2503).
Other Directives: Delaware Advance Directive contains Power of Attorney for Health Care and Instructions for Health Care (Section 16-2503). Anatomical Gift Act (Sections 16-2710 - 16-2719). Durable Power of Attorney (Section 12-4901 - 12-4905).
Living Will Effective: Two (2) physicians determine in writing that you have a terminal condition and/or are in a permanent state of unconsciousness.
Witness Requirements: Sign in the presence of two (2) adult witnesses. A witness cannot be a person who has claim against your estate upon your death, stands to inherit from your estate, be directly financially responsible for your health care, or be an owner, operator, or employee of a residential long-term health care institution in which you reside. If declarant is a patient in a nursing home, one of the witnesses must be a patient advocate or ombudsman.

District of Columbia (Washington D.C.)

State Website: http://dccode.westgroup.com/home/dccodes/default.wl
State Law Reference: District of Columbia Code Annotated.
Living Will Form: District of Columbia Declaration serves as Living Will (Section 7-622).
Other Directives: Power of Attorney for Health Care (Section 212207). Anatomical Gift Act (Section 7-1521.04). Durable Power of Attorney (Section 21-2081).
Living Will Effective: Two (2) physicians determine that you are in a terminal condition and your death will result without using life sustaining procedures. Your physician must then record your diagnosis and the contents of your Declaration in your medical records.
Witness Requirements: Sign in the presence of two (2) adult witnesses. A witness cannot be your appointed attorney in fact, health care provider, or an employee of your health care provider. Witnesses also cannot be related by blood, marriage, or adoption, stand to inherit from your estate, or be financially responsible for your health care.

Florida

State Website: http://www.flsenate.gov/statutes/index.cfm
State Law Reference: Florida Statutes Annotated.
Living Will Form: Living Will (Section 765-303).
Other Directives: Designation of Health Care Surrogate (Section 765203). Anatomical Gift Act (Sections 765.510 - 765.546). Durable Power of Attorney (Section 709.08).
Living Will Effective: Two (2) physicians determine in writing that you have a terminal condition, and/or are in a permanent state of unconsciousness and can no longer make your own health care decisions.
Witness Requirements: Sign in the presence of two (2) adult witnesses. At least one (1) of your witnesses must not be related to you by marriage or blood.

Georgia

State Website: www.legis.state.ga.us
State Law Reference: Code of Georgia Annotated.
Living Will Form: Georgia Living Will (Section 31-32-3).
Other Directives: Durable Power of Attorney For Health Care (Section 31361). Anatomical Gift Act Section 44-4-140). Durable Power of Attorney (Sections 10-6-140 through 10-6-142).
Living Will Effective: Two (2) physicians determine in writing that you have a terminal condition, and/or are in a permanent state of unconsciousness.
Witness Requirements: Sign in the presence of two (2) adult witnesses. A witness cannot be a person who has claim against your estate upon your death, stands to inherit from your estate, be directly financially responsible for your health care, or be an owner, operator, or employee of a health care institution in which you are a patient. Witnesses also cannot be related by blood or marriage.

Hawaii

State Website: http://www.capitol.hawaii.gov/
State Law Reference: Hawaii Revised Statutes.
Living Will Form: Instruction for Health Care serves as Living Will (Section 327E-3).
Other Directives: Hawaii Advanced Health Care Directive has Durable Power of Attorney for Health Care and Instructions for Health Care (Section 327E3). Anatomical Gift Act (Section 327-1). Durable Power of Attorney (Sections 551D-1 through 551D-7).
Living Will Effective: In the event that you have an incurable and irreversible condition that will result in death within a relatively short time, become unconscious and, to a reasonable degree of medical certainty, will not regain consciousness, or the likely risks and burdens of treatment would outweigh the expected benefits.
Witness Requirements: Sign in the presence of two (2) adult witnesses. At least one (1) of your witnesses cannot be related to you by marriage or blood or entitled to any part of your estate. A witness cannot be the person you appoint as your agent, health care provider, or an employee of your health care provider.

Idaho

State Website: http://www3.state.id.us/
State Law Reference: Idaho Code.
Living Will Form: Idaho Living Will (Section 39-4504).
Other Directives: Durable Power of Attorney for Health Care (Section 394505). Anatomical Gift Act (Section 39-3413). Durable Power of Attorney (Section 15-5-503).
Living Will Effective: Two (2) physicians determine that you are in a terminal condition, your death will result without using life sustaining procedures, or you are in a persistent vegetative state.
Witness Requirements: Sign in the presence of two (2) adult witnesses. No other restrictions apply.

Illinois

State Website: http://www.ilga.gov/

State Law Reference: Illinois Compiled Statutes.

Living Will Form: Illinois Declaration serves as Living Will (Section 755-35/1).

Other Directives: Durable Power of Attorney for Health Care (Section 75545/4-1). Anatomical Gift Act (Section 755-50). Durable Power of Attorney (Section 755-45/2-1).

Living Will Effective: If death would occur without the use of death delaying procedures. Your physician must personally examine you and certify in writing that you are terminally ill.

Witness Requirements: Sign in the presence of two (2) adult witnesses. Witnesses cannot be entitled to any part of your estate or financially responsible for your medical care.

Indiana

State Website: http://www.in.gov/legislative/ic/code/

State Law Reference: Indiana Code Annotated.

Living Will Form: Indiana Living Will Declaration (Section 16-36-4-10).

Other Directives: Durable Power of Attorney for Health Care Decisions and Appointment of Health Care Representative are contained within the Living Will document. Anatomical Gift Act (Section 29-2-16-1). Durable Power of Attorney (Section 29-3-5).

Living Will Effective: Your physician must certify in writing that you are in a terminal condition and your death would occur within a short period of time without the use of life sustaining medical care.

Witness Requirements: Sign in the presence of two (2) adult witnesses. Witnesses cannot be entitled to any part of your estate, related to you by blood or marriage, financially responsible for your medical care, or be the person who signed the Declaration on your behalf.

Iowa

State Website: http://www.legis.state.ia.us/

State Law Reference: Iowa Code Annotated.

Living Will Form: Iowa Declaration serves as Living Will (Section 144A.3).

Other Directives: Durable Power of Attorney for Health Care (Section 144B.2). Anatomical Gift Act (Section 142C). Durable Power of Attorney (Section 633.705).

Living Will Effective: Two (2) physicians must certify in writing that you are in a terminal condition and your death would occur within a short period of time without the use of life sustaining medical care.

Witness Requirements: Sign in the presence of two (2) witnesses eighteen (18) years or older or a notary public. A witness cannot be your health care provider or an employee of your health care provider.

Kansas

State Website: http://www.kslegislature.org/

State Law Reference: Kansas Statutes Annotated.

Living Will Form: Kansas Declaration serves as Living Will (Section 65-28103).

Other Directives: Durable Power of Attorney for Health Care (Section 58629). Anatomical Gift Act (Section 65-3209). Durable Power of Attorney (Section 58-629).

Living Will Effective: Two (2) physicians must certify in writing that you are in a terminal condition and your death would occur within a short period of time without the use of life sustaining medical care.

Witness Requirements: Sign in the presence of two (2) witnesses eighteen (18) years or older or a notary public. Witnesses cannot be entitled to any part of your estate, be financially responsible for your medical care, be related to you by blood or marriage, or be the person who signed the Declaration on your behalf.

Kentucky

State Website: http://lrc.ky.gov/

State Law Reference: Kentucky Revised Statutes.

Living Will Form: Living Will Directive (Section 311.625).

Other Directives: Anatomical Gift Act (Sections 311.165 through 311.235). Durable Power of Attorney (Section 386.093).

Living Will Effective: When you become unable to make your own medical decisions.

Witness Requirements: Sign in the presence of two (2) witnesses eighteen (18) years or older or a notary public. Witnesses cannot be entitled to any part of your estate, financially responsible for your medical care, or related to you by blood or marriage.

Louisiana

State Website: http://www.legis.state.la.us/

State Law Reference: Louisiana Revised Statutes and Louisiana Civil Code Annotated.

Living Will Form: Louisiana Declaration serves as Living Will (Title 40, Article 1299, Section 583).

Other Directives: Anatomical Gift Act (Section 17:2354).

Living Will Effective: Two (2) physicians must certify in writing that you are in a terminal condition and your death would occur within a short period of time without the use of life sustaining medical care.

Witness Requirements: Sign in the presence of two (2) adult witnesses. Witnesses cannot be entitled to any part of your estate or related by blood or marriage.

Maine

State Website: http://janus.state.me.us/legis/statutes/

State Law Reference: Maine Revised Statutes Annotated.

Living Will Form: Instructions for Health Care serves as Living Will (Section 18A-5-8040).

Other Directives: Durable Power of Attorney for Health Care (Section 185506). Anatomical Gift Act (Section 22-2-710). Durable Power of Attorney (Section 18A-5-502).

Living Will Effective: The Living Will becomes effective in the event that you have an incurable and irreversible condition that will result in death within a relatively short time, become unconscious and, to a reasonable degree of medical certainty, will not regain consciousness, or the likely risks and burdens of treatment would outweigh the expected benefits.

Witness Requirements: Sign in the presence of two (2) adult witnesses. No other restrictions apply.

Maryland

State Website: http://198.187.128.12/maryland/lpext.dll?f=templates&fn=fs-main.htm&2.0

State Law Reference: Maryland Code.

Living Will Form: Advance Medical Directive Health Care Instructions serve as Living Will (Health General, Section 5-603).

Other Directives: Appointment of Health Care Agent (Health General, Section 5603). Anatomical Gift Act (Health General 5-604.1). Durable Power of Attorney (Estates & Trusts 13-601).

Living Will Effective: Two (2) physicians must agree in writing that you are incapable of making an informed health care decision, but you are not unconscious or unable to communicate by any other means.

Witness Requirements: Sign in the presence of two (2) adult witnesses. The person you assign as your agent cannot be a witness. At least one (1) of your witnesses must be a person who is not entitled to any portion of your estate or financial benefit by reason of your death.

Massachusetts

State Website: http://www.mass.gov/legis/laws/mgl/

State Law Reference: Massachusetts General Laws.

Living Will Form: No state statute governing the use of Living Wills. However, you have a constitutional right to state your wishes about medical care. A form is provided in this book.

Other Directives: Massachusetts Health Care Proxy. (Chapter 201D, Sections 1-17)

Living Will Effective: In the event that you develop an irreversible condition that prevents you from making your own medical decisions.

Witness Requirements: Because Massachusetts does not have a statute governing the use of Living Wills, there are no specific requirements to make your Living Will legally binding. We suggest that you sign in the presence of two (2) witnesses eighteen (18) years or older or a notary public. A witness should not be your health care provider or an employee of your health care provider. Witnesses should not be entitled to any part of your estate, financially responsible for your medical care, or related to you by blood or marriage.

Michigan

State Website: http://www.michiganlegislature.org/

State Law Reference: Michigan Compiled Laws Annotated.

Living Will Form: No state statute governing the use of Living Wills. However, you have a constitutional right to state your wishes about medical care. A form is provided in this book.

Other Directives: Michigan Designation of Patient Advocate for Health Care. (Section 700.5506).

Living Will Effective: In the event that you develop an irreversible condition that prevents you from making your own medical decisions.

Witness Requirements: Because Michigan does not have a statute governing the use of Living Wills, there are no specific requirements to make your Living Will legally binding. We suggest that you sign in the presence of two (2) witnesses eighteen (18) years or older or a notary public. A witness should not be your health care provider or an employee of your health care provider. Witnesses should not be entitled to any part of your estate, be financially responsible for your medical care, or be related to you by blood or marriage.

Minnesota

State Website: http://www.revisor.leg.state.mn.us/stats/

State Law Reference: Minnesota Statutes Annotated.

Living Will Form: Health Care Living Will (Chapter 145B, Section 04).

Other Directives: Appointment of Health Care Agent is included in Living Will (Section 145B-04). Anatomical Gift Act (Section 145B.07). Durable Power of Attorney (Section 523.01).

Living Will Effective: Living Will becomes effective in the event that you can no longer make your own medical decisions.

Witness Requirements: Sign in the presence of two (2) witnesses eighteen (18) years or older or a notary public. A witness cannot be the person whom you appointed as your agent. At least one (1) witness cannot be your health care provider or an employee of your health care provider.

Mississippi

State Website: http://www.mscode.com/

State Law Reference: Mississippi Code Annotated.

Living Will Form: Instructions for Health Care serves as Living Will (Title 41, Chapter 41, Section 209).

Other Directives: Mississippi Advance Health Care Directive contains Power of Attorney for Health Care and Instructions for Health Care (Section 41-209). Anatomical Gift Act (Sections 41-39-31 through 41-39-51). Durable Power of Attorney (Section 87-3-1).

Living Will Effective: In the event that you have an incurable and irreversible condition that will result in death within a relatively short time, become unconscious and, to a reasonable degree of medical certainty, will not regain consciousness, or the likely risks and burdens of treatment would outweigh the expected benefits.

Witness Requirements: Sign in the presence of two (2) witnesses eighteen

(18) years or older or a notary public. A witness cannot be the person whom you appointed as your agent, health care provider, or an employee of your health care provider. At least one (1) witness cannot be related to you by blood or marriage or entitled to your estate upon your death.

Missouri

State Website: http://www.moga.state.mo.us/STATUTES/STATUTES.HTM#T

State Law Reference: Missouri Annotated Statutes.

Living Will Form: Missouri Declaration serves as Living Will (Chapter 459, Section 015).

Other Directives: Power of Attorney for Health Care (Section 404822). Anatomical Gift Act (Sections 194.210 through 194290). Durable Power of Attorney (Section 404.705).

Living Will Effective: The Declaration becomes effective in the event that you have an incurable or irreversible medical condition which, without the use of life support, will result in death in a relative short period of time, or you are in a permanent coma or persistent vegetative state.

Witness Requirements: Sign in the presence of two (2) adult witnesses. If you have someone sign the Declaration on your behalf, that person cannot serve as a witness.

Montana

State Website: http://data.opi.state.mt.us/bills/mca_toc/index.htm

State Law Reference: Montana Code Annotated.

Living Will Form: Montana Declaration serves as Living Will (Title 50, Chapter 9, Section 103).

Other Directives: Appointment of Health Care Agent is included in Declaration (Section 50-9-103). Anatomical Gift Act (Section 72-17-101). Durable Power of Attorney (Section 72-5-501).

Living Will Effective: Becomes effective when you have an incurable or irreversible medical condition which, without the use of life support, will result in death in a relatively short period of time, or you are in a permanent coma or persistent vegetative state.

Witness Requirements: Sign in the presence of two (2) adult witnesses. No other restrictions apply. Do not use your appointed health care agent as one of your witnesses.

Nebraska

State Website: http://statutes.unicam.state.ne.us/

State Law Reference: Revised Statutes of Nebraska.

Living Will Form: Nebraska Declaration serves as Living Will (Chapter 20, Section 404).

Other Directives: Power of Attorney for Health Care (Section 303408). Anatomical Gift Act (Section 71-4804). Durable Power of Attorney (Section 30-2665).

Living Will Effective: Declaration becomes effective when your attending physician determines you to have an incurable or irreversible medical condition which, without the use of life support, will result in death in a relatively short period of time, or you are in a permanent coma or persistent vegetative state.

Witness Requirements: Sign in the presence of two (2) adult witnesses. Witnesses cannot be employees of your life or health insurance provider and at least one (1) witness must not be an administrator or employee of your treating health care provider

Nevada

State Website: http://www.leg.state.nv.us/NRS/

State Law Reference: Nevada Revised Statutes Annotated.

Living Will Form: Nevada Declaration serves as Living Will (Section 449-610).

Other Directives: Power of Attorney for Health Care (Section 449830). Anatomical Gift Act (Sections 451.500 through 451590).

Living Will Effective: Declaration becomes effective when your doctor determines that your death would occur without the use of life-sustaining medical care.

Witness Requirements: Sign in the presence of two (2) adult witnesses. No other restrictions apply

New Hampshire

State Website: http://gencourt.state.nh.us/rsa/html/indexes/default.asp
State Law Reference: New Hampshire Revised Statutes.
Living Will Form: New Hampshire Declaration serves as Living Will (Chapter 137H, Section 3).
Other Directives: Power of Attorney for Health Care (Chapter 137J:15). Anatomical Gift Act (Chapter 291-A).
Living Will Effective: Two (2) physicians must certify in writing that you are in a terminal condition and your death would occur within a short period of time without the use of life-sustaining medical care.
Witness Requirements: Sign in the presence of two (2) witnesses eighteen (18) years or older or a notary public. A witness cannot be a person who has a claim against your estate, stands to inherit from your estate, be your spouse, or be your doctor or a person acting under direction or control of your doctor. If you are a resident of a health care facility or a patient in a hospital, one of your witnesses may be your doctor or an employee of your doctor.

New Jersey

State Website: http://www.njleg.state.nj.us
State Law Reference: New Jersey Revised Statutes.
Living Will Form: New Jersey Instruction Directive serves as Living Will (Section 26-2H-55).
Other Directives: Appointment of a Health Care Representative (Section 262H58). Anatomical Gift Act (Section 26:6-65). Durable Power of Attorney (Section 3B:13a-10).
Living Will Effective: Your doctor or treating health care institution must receive this document. Your attending physician and one (1) other physician must confirm that you are unable to make health care decisions.
Witness Requirements: Sign in the presence of two (2) witnesses eighteen (18) years or older or a notary public. A witness cannot be the person whom you appointed as your agent.

New Mexico

State Website: http://www.legis.state.nm.us/
State Law Reference: New Mexico Statutes Annotated.
Living Will Form: Optional Advance Health Care Directive (Section 24-7A-4).
Other Directives: Power of Attorney for Health Care (Section 247A4). Anatomical Gift Act (Sections 24-6A-1 through 42-6A-15). Durable Power of Attorney (Sections 45-5-501 through 45-5-505).
Living Will Effective: This document becomes effective in the event that you have an incurable and irreversible condition that will result in death within a relatively short time, become unconscious and, to a reasonable degree of medical certainty, will not regain consciousness, or the likely risks and burdens of treatment would outweigh the expected benefits.
Witness Requirements: The law does not require that your advance directive be witnessed. To avoid future concerns, we recommend that you sign in the presence of two (2) witnesses eighteen (18) years or older or a notary public. A witness should not be the person whom you appointed as your agent.

New York

State Website: http://assembly.state.ny.us/leg/
State Law Reference: New York Consolidated Laws.
Living Will Form: Order not to resuscitate acts as Living Will. (Health Care, Article 29-B, Sections 2960 -2979).
Other Directives: Health Care Proxy (Chapter 45, Article 29C, Section 2980). Anatomical Gift Act (Sections 45-43-4300 through 45-43-4309). Durable Power of Attorney (Sections 24A-5-1501 through 24A-5-1506).
Living Will Effective: The Living Will becomes effective when you become terminally ill, permanently unconscious, or minimally conscious due to brain damage and will never regain the ability to make decisions.
Witness Requirements: Order not to resuscitate acts as Living Will in New York. You must sign in the presence of two (2) adult witnesses who do not benefit from your estate.

North Carolina

State Website: http://www.ncga.state.nc.us/
State Law Reference: North Carolina General Statutes.
Living Will Form: Declaration of a Desire for a Natural Death serves as Living Will (Section 9023321).
Other Directives: Health Care Power of Attorney (Section 32A- 2- 25). Anatomical Gift Act (Section 130A-402). Durable Power of Attorney (Section 32A-8 through 32A-14).
Living Will Effective: Two (2) physicians must certify in writing that you are in a terminal condition and your death would occur within a short period of time without the use of life-sustaining medical care.
Witness Requirements: Sign in the presence of two (2) adult witnesses and a notary public. A witness cannot be a person who has claim against your estate upon your death, stands to inherit from your estate, be directly financially responsible for your health care, or be an owner, operator, or employee of a health care institution in which you are a patient. Witnesses also cannot be related by blood or marriage.

North Dakota

State Website: http://www.state.nd.us/lr/information/statutes/centcode.html
State Law Reference: North Dakota Century Code.
Living Will Form: Declaration serves as Living Will (Chapter 23, Section 6.4).
Other Directives: Power of Attorney for Health Care (Section 2306.5). Anatomical Gift Act (Sections 23-06.2-01 through 23-06.2-12). Durable Power of Attorney (Section 30.1-30).
Living Will Effective: Two (2) physicians must certify in writing that you are in a terminal condition and your death would occur within a short period of time without the use of lifesustaining medical care.
Witness Requirements: Sign in the presence of two (2) adult witnesses and a notary public. A witness cannot be a person who has claim against your estate upon your death, stands to inherit from your estate, be directly financially responsible for your health care, or be your doctor. Witnesses also cannot be related by blood or marriage. If you are presently living in a nursing home or other longterm care facility, one (1) of your witnesses must be one (1) of the following: a member of the clergy, a lawyer licensed to practice in North Dakota, or a person designated by the Department of Human Services or the county court for the county in which the facility is located

Ohio

State Website: http://onlinedocs.andersonpublishing.com/revisedcode/
State Law Reference: Ohio Revised Code Annotated.
Living Will Form: Living Will Declaration (Title 37, Chapter 2133, Section 04).
Other Directives: Power of Attorney for Health Care (Section 1337-12). Anatomical Gift Act (Section 2108.09). Durable Power of Attorney (Section 1337-01).
Living Will Effective: Two (2) physicians determine that you are in a terminal condition and your death will result without using lifesustaining procedures, including the determination that there is no reasonable possibility that you will regain the ability to make your own health care decisions.
Witness Requirements: Sign in front of two (2) witnesses eighteen (18)

years or older or a notary public. Witnesses cannot be related to you by blood, marriage, or adoption, or be your doctor or the administrator of a nursing home in which you are receiving treatment.

Oklahoma
State Website: http://www.oscn.net/
State Law Reference: Oklahoma Statutes Annotated.
Living Will Form: Is Part 1 of Advance Directive for Health Care (Title 63, Article 3101, Section 4).
Other Directives: Appointment of Health Care Proxy is Part 2 of Advance Directive for Health Care (Section 633101.4). Anatomical Gift Act (Sections 63-2201 through 63-2209). Durable Power of Attorney (Sections 15-1001 through 15-1020).
Living Will Effective: This Directive goes into effect once it is given to your doctor and you are unable to make your own medical decisions. In order to follow your instructions regarding life-sustaining treatment, your doctor must first consult another doctor to determine that you are persistently unconscious or suffering from a terminal condition.
Witness Requirements: Sign in the presence of two (2) adult witnesses. A witness cannot be any person who would inherit from you under any existing will or by operation of law.

Oregon
State Website: http://www.leg.state.or.us/ors/
State Law Reference: Oregon Revised Statutes.
Living Will Form: Health Care Instructions serves as Living Will (Chapter 127, Section 531).
Other Directives: Appointment of Health Care Representative (Section 127531). Anatomical Gift Act (Sections 97.950 through 97.964). Durable Power of Attorney (Section 127.005).
Living Will Effective: Two (2) physicians agree that you have an incurable and irreversible condition that will result in death within a relatively short time, will become unconscious and, to a reasonable degree of medical certainty, will not regain consciousness, or the likely risks and burdens of treatment would outweigh the expected benefits.
Witness Requirements: Sign in the presence of two (2) adult witnesses. If you have someone sign the Declaration on your behalf, that person cannot serve as a witness. Your attending physician cannot be a witness. At least one (1) of your witnesses cannot be related to you by blood, marriage, or adoption, entitled to any portion of your estate, or be an owner, operator, or employee of your treating health care facility.

Pennsylvania
State Website: http://members.aol.com/StatutesPA/Index.html
State Law Reference: Pennsylvania Code.
Living Will Form: Declaration serves as Living Will. (Section 20-5404).
Other Directives: Anatomical Gift Act (Section 20-8613).
Living Will Effective: The Declaration becomes effective when your physician receives a copy of it and determines that you are incompetent and in a terminal condition or a state of permanent unconsciousness.
Witness Requirements: Sign in the presence of two (2) adult witnesses. If you have someone sign the Declaration on your behalf, that person cannot serve as a witness.

Rhode Island
State Website: http://www.rilin.state.ri.us/Statutes/Statutes.html
State Law Reference: Rhode Island General Laws.
Living Will Form: Declaration serves as Living Will (Chapter 23, Article 4, Section 113).
Other Directives: Power of Attorney for Health Care (Section 234.10). Anatomical Gift Act (Section 23-18.6). Durable Power of Attorney (Section 18-3-5).
Living Will Effective: Your doctor must determine that your death would

occur without use of life sustaining medical care.
Witness Requirements: Sign in the presence of two (2) adult witnesses. Witnesses cannot be related to you by blood, marriage, or adoption.

South Carolina
State Website: http://www.scstatehouse.net/code/statmast.htm/
State Law Reference: Code of Laws of South Carolina Annotated.
Living Will Form: Declaration of a Desire for a Natural Death serves as Living Will (Title 44, Chapter 77, Section 50).
Other Directives: Health Care Power of Attorney (Section 625501). Anatomical Gift Act (Sections 44-43-10 through 44-43-50). Durable Power of Attorney (Section 62-5-501).
Living Will Effective: Two (2) physicians must determine you are in a terminal condition and your death will result without using life-sustaining procedures.
Witness Requirements: Sign in the presence of two (2) adult witnesses and a notary public. A witness cannot be a beneficiary of your life insurance policy, your health care provider, or an employee of your health care provider. Witnesses cannot be related to you by blood, marriage, or adoption, entitled to any part of your estate, or directly financially responsible for your health care. In addition, at least one (1) witness must not be an employee of a health facility in which you are a patient. If you are a resident in a hospital or nursing facility, one of the witnesses must also be an ombudsman designated by the State Ombudsman, Office of the Governor.

South Dakota
State Website: http://legis.state.sd.us/statutes/
State Law Reference: South Dakota Codified Laws Annotated.
Living Will Form: Living Will Declaration (Title 34, Chapter 12D, Section 3).
Other Directives: Power of Attorney for Health Care (Section 3412C). Anatomical Gift Act (Sections 34-26-20 through 34-26-47). Durable Power of Attorney (Section 51A-11-4).
Living Will Effective: Declaration is effective when your death will result without using life-sustaining procedures, including the determination that there is no reasonable possibility that you will regain the ability to make your own health care decisions.
Witness Requirements: Sign in the presence of two (2) witnesses eighteen (18) years or older or a notary public. Although South Dakota does not have any restrictions on who can be a witness, we suggest that you not use your appointed attorney-in-fact or your health care provider.

Tennessee
State Website: http://www.michie.com
State Law Reference: Tennessee Code Annotated.
Living Will Form: Living Will (Section 32-22-105).
Other Directives: Power of Attorney for Health Care (Section 346204). Anatomical Gift Act (Section 68-30-10). Durable Power of Attorney (Section 34-6-204).
Living Will Effective: The Living Will becomes effective when your death will result without using life-sustaining procedures.
Witness Requirements: Sign in the presence of two (2) adult witnesses and a notary public. A witness cannot be a person who has claim against your estate upon your death, stands to inherit from your estate, be your doctor or an employee of your doctor, or be an owner, operator, or employee of a health care institution in which you are a patient. Witnesses also cannot be related by blood or marriage.

Texas
State Website: www.capitol.state.tx.us
State Law Reference: Texas Statutes and Code Annotated.
Living Will Form: Directive to Physicians and Family or Surrogate serves as Living Will (Health & Safety Code 166-033).
Other Directives: Medical Power of Attorney (Health & Safety Code

12481). Anatomical Gift Act Texas (Health & Safety Code 166-152). Durable Power of Attorney (Probate Code 482).

Living Will Effective: This Directive becomes effective when your attending physician certifies in writing that you are in a terminal or irreversible condition.

Witness Requirements: At least one (1) witness cannot be related to you by blood, marriage, or adoption, designated to make treatment decisions for you, entitled to any part of your estate, or be your doctor or an employee of your doctor. A witness cannot be an employee of a health care facility in which you are a patient, an officer, director, partner, or a business office employee of the health care facility or any part of any parent organization of the health care facility, or have a claim against your estate after you die.

Utah

State Website: http://www.le.state.ut.us/

State Law Reference: Utah Code Annotated.

Living Will Form: Directive to Physicians and Providers of Medical Services serves as Living Will, (Section 75-2-1104).

Other Directives: Special Power of Attorney for Health Care (Section 7521106). Anatomical Gift Act (Section 26-28-3). Durable Power of Attorney (Section 75-5-501).

Living Will Effective: Two (2) physicians must physically examine you and certify in writing you are in a terminal condition or persistent vegetative state.

Witness Requirements: Sign in the presence of two (2) witnesses eighteen (18) years or older. A witness cannot be entitled to any part of your estate, be financially responsible for your medical care, be related to you by blood or marriage, be the person who signed the Declaration on your behalf, or be an employee of your health care facility.

Vermont

State Website: http://www.leg.state.vt.us/statutes/statutes2.htm

State Law Reference: Vermont Statutes Annotated.

Living Will Form: Terminal Care Document serves as Living Will (Section 18-5253).

Other Directives: Power of Attorney for Health Care (Section 18-5276). Anatomical Gift Act (Section 18-109). Durable Power of Attorney (Section 14-3508).

Living Will Effective: Document becomes effective if death would occur regardless of the use of lifesustaining procedures.

Witness Requirements: Sign in the presence of two (2) witnesses eighteen (18) years or older. A witness cannot be entitled to any part of your estate, be your spouse, attending physician or any person acting under the direction or control of your attending physician, or any person who has a claim against your estate.

Virginia

State Website: http://leg1.state.va.us/

State Law Reference: Virginia Code Annotated.

Living Will Form: Advance Medical Directive serves as Living Will (Section 54.1-29-84).

Other Directives: Anatomical Gift Act (Section 32.1-8-290). Durable Power of Attorney (Sections 37.1-4-134.8 through 37.1-4-137.1).

Living Will Effective: This directive becomes effective in the event that you develop a terminal condition or are in a permanent vegetative state and can no longer make your own medical decisions.

Witness Requirements: Sign in the presence of two (2) witnesses eighteen (18) years or older. Witnesses cannot be related by blood or marriage.

Washington

State Website: http://www.leg.wa.gov/

State Law Reference: Washington Revised Code Annotated.

Living Will Form: Health Care Directive serves as Living Will (Section 70.22.030).

Other Directives: Power of Attorney for Health Care (Section 11.94.010). Anatomical Gift Act (Section 68.50.540). Durable Power of Attorney (Sections 11.94.101 through 11.94.900).

Living Will Effective: Declaration applies when two (2) physicians diagnose you to have a incurable or irreversible condition that will cause death in a relatively short time and you can no longer make your own medical decisions.

Witness Requirements: Sign in the presence of two (2) witnesses eighteen (18) years or older. A witness cannot be entitled to any part of your estate, related by blood or marriage, be your attending physician or any person acting under the direction or control of your attending physician, or be any person who has a claim against your estate.

West Virginia

State Website: http://www.legis.state.wv.us/

State Law Reference: West Virginia Code Annotated.

Living Will Form: Living Will, (Section 16-30-4).

Other Directives: Medical Power of Attorney (Section 16304). Anatomical Gift Act (Section 16-19-2). Durable Power of Attorney (Sections 39-4-1 through 39-4-7).

Living Will Effective: Your physician must certify in writing that you are in a terminal condition and your death would occur within a short period of time without the use of life-sustaining medical care.

Witness Requirements: Sign in the presence of two (2) adult witnesses and a notary public. A witness cannot be a person who stands to inherit from your estate, be directly financially responsible for your health care, be your attending physician, or be your health care representative or successor if you have a medical power of attorney. A witness cannot be related by blood or marriage or be the person who signed the document on your behalf.

Wisconsin

State Website: http://www.legis.state.wi.us/

State Law Reference: Wisconsin Statutes Annotated.

Living Will Form: Declaration to Physicians serves as Living Will (Section 154-03).

Other Directives: Power of Attorney for Health Care (Section 15505). Anatomical Gift Act (Section 157.06). Durable Power of Attorney (Section 243.07-1a).

Living Will Effective: This directive becomes effective in the event that your attending physician and one (1) other physician certifies you have developed a terminal condition or are in a permanent vegetative state and can no longer make your own medical decisions.

Witness Requirements: Sign in the presence of two (2) adult witnesses. A witness cannot be a person who stands to inherit from your estate, be directly financially responsible for your health care, be your attending physician, or be an employee of your health care provider or an inpatient health care facility in which you are a patient, unless the employee is a chaplain or social worker. A witness also cannot be related by blood or marriage.

Wyoming

State Website: http://legisweb.state.wy.us/

State Law Reference: Wyoming Statutes.

Living Will Form: Living Will Declaration (Section 35-22-102).

Other Directives: Power of Attorney for Health Care (Section 35201). Anatomical Gift Act (Section 35-5-102). Durable Power of Attorney (Section 3-5-101).

Living Will Effective: This Declaration becomes effective when two (2) physicians agree that you have a terminal condition from which there can be no recovery and your death is imminent.

Witness Requirements: Sign in the presence of two (2) witnesses eighteen (18) years or older or a notary public. Witnesses cannot be entitled to any part of your estate or financially responsible for your medical care. A witness cannot be related to you by blood or marriage or be the person who signed the Declaration on your behalf.

Revocation of Living Will

I, _____ , am the Declarant and maker of a Living Will, dated _____ ,
20_____ .

By this written revocation, I hereby entirely revoke such Living Will and intend that it no longer
have any force or effect whatsoever.

Dated _____ , 20_____ .

_____
Declarant's Signature

_____
Printed Name of Declarant

_____
Signature of Witness #1

_____
Printed name of Witness #1

_____
Address of Witness #1

_____
Signature of Witness #2

_____
Printed name of Witness #2

_____
Address of Witness #2

Revocation of Health Care Power of Attorney

I, _____ , residing at _____ ,

City of _____ , State of _____ , revoke the Health Care Power of Attor-

ney dated _____ , 20_____ , which was granted to _____ , residing

at _____ , City of _____ ,

State of _____ , to act as my attorney-in-fact for health care decisions and I revoke

any appointment of the above person as my health care agent, health care representative, or health

care proxy.

Dated _____ , 20___

_____
Signature of person revoking power of attorney

_____
Printed name of person revoking power of attorney

_____
Signature of Witness #1

_____
Printed name of Witness #1

_____
Address of Witness #1

_____
Signature of Witness #2

_____
Printed name of Witness #2

_____
Address of Witness #2

Alabama Living Will

This form may be used in the State of Alabama to make your wishes known about what medical treatment or other care you would or would not want if you become too sick to speak for yourself. You are not required to have an advance directive. If you do have an advance directive, be sure that your doctor, family, and friends know you have one and know where it is located.

I, _____, being of sound mind and at least 19 years old, would like to make the following wishes known. I direct that my family, my doctors and health care workers, and all others follow the directions I am writing down. I know that at any time I can change my mind about these directions by tearing up this form and writing a new one. I can also do away with these directions by tearing them up and by telling someone at least 19 years of age of my wishes and asking him or her to write them down. I understand that these directions will only be used if I am not able to speak for myself.

If I Become Terminally Ill or Injured:

Terminally ill or injured is when my doctor and another doctor decide that I have a condition that cannot be cured and that I will likely die in the near future from this condition.

Life sustaining treatment: Life sustaining treatment includes drugs, machines, or medical procedures that would keep me alive but would not cure me. I know that even if I choose not to have life sustaining treatment, I will still get medicines and treatments that ease my pain and keep me comfortable.

Place your initials by either "yes" or "no":
_____ Yes _____ No I want to have life sustaining treatment if I am terminally ill or injured.

Artificially provided food and hydration (Food and water through a tube or an IV): I understand that if I am terminally ill or injured I may need to be given food and water through a tube or an IV to keep me alive if I can no longer chew or swallow on my own or with someone helping me.

Place your initials by either "yes" or "no":
_____ Yes _____ No I want to have food and water provided through a tube or an IV if I am terminally ill or injured.

If I Become Permanently Unconscious:

Permanent unconsciousness is when my doctor and another doctor agree that within a reasonable degree of medical certainty I can no longer think, feel anything, knowingly move, or be aware of being alive. They believe this condition will last indefinitely without hope for improvement and have watched me long enough to make that decision. I understand that at least one of these doctors must be qualified to make such a diagnosis.

Life sustaining treatment: Life sustaining treatment includes drugs, machines, or other medical procedures that would keep me alive but would not cure me. I know that even if I choose not to have life sustaining treatment, I will still get medicines and treatments that ease my pain and keep me comfortable.

Place your initials by either "yes" or "no":
_____ Yes _____ No I want to have life-sustaining treatment if I am permanently unconscious.

Artificially provided food and hydration (Food and water through a tube or an IV): I understand that if I become permanently unconscious, I may need to be given food and water through a tube or an IV to keep me alive if I can no longer chew or swallow on my own or with someone helping me.

Place your initials by either "yes" or "no":
_____ Yes _____ No I want to have food and water provided through a tube or an IV if I am permanently unconscious.

Other Directions:

Please list any other things you want done or not done. In addition to the directions I have listed on this form, I also want the following:

If you do not have other directions, place your initials below:
_____ No, I do not have any other directions.

I understand the following:

If my doctor or hospital does not want to follow the directions I have listed, they must see that I get to a doctor or hospital who will follow my directions.

If I am pregnant, or if I become pregnant, the choices I have made on this form will not be followed until after the birth of the baby.

If the time comes for me to stop receiving life sustaining treatment or food and water through a tube or an IV, I direct that my doctor talk about the good and bad points of doing this, along with my wishes, with my health care proxy, if I have one, and with the following people:

My signature

Your printed name: _____

The month, day, and year of your birth: _____

Your signature: _____

Date signed: _____

Witnesses (need two witnesses to sign)

I am witnessing this form because I believe this person to be of sound mind. I did not sign the person's signature, and I am not the health care proxy. I am not related to the person by blood, adoption, or marriage and not entitled to any part of his or her estate. I am at least 19 years of age and am not directly responsible for paying for his or her medical care.

Printed name of first witness: _____

Signature: _____

Date: _____

Printed name of second witness: _____

Signature: _____

Date: _____

Alaska Living Will

If I should have an incurable or irreversible condition that will cause my death within a relatively short time, it is my desire that my life not be prolonged by administration of life-sustaining procedures. If my condition is terminal and I am unable to participate in decisions regarding my medical treatment, I direct my attending physician to withhold or withdraw procedures that merely prolong the dying process and are not necessary to my comfort or to alleviate pain. (Initial your choice).

[   ] I DO desire that nutrition or hydration (food and water) be provided by gastric tube or intravenously if necessary.

[   ] I DO NOT desire that nutrition or hydration (food and water) be provided by gastric tube or intravenously if necessary.

Notwithstanding the other provisions of this declaration, if I have donated an organ and if I am in a hospital when a "do not resuscitate" order is to be implemented for me, I do not want the "do not resuscitate" order to take effect until the donated organ can be evaluated to determine if the organ is suitable for donation.

Signed this _____ day of _____, _____.

Signature _____

Printed Name _____

Place _____

If another person is to sign for the declarant at the declarant's direction, the person signing for the declarant must sign in the presence of two persons or a person who is qualified to take acknowledgments under AS 09.63.010. The witness form below may be used for the two witnesses. The acknowledgment form below may be used for the person qualified to take acknowledgments.

Witness Form

Witness Signature _____

Printed Name _____

Address _____

Witness Signature _____

Printed Name _____

Address _____

Or Acknowledgment Form (on reverse side)

State of Alaska

_____ Judicial District

The foregoing instrument was acknowledged before me this (date) _____ by _____
(name of person who acknowledged).

_____

Signature of Person Taking Acknowledgment

_____ Title or Rank

_____ Serial Number, if any.

Arizona Living Will

Some general statements concerning your health care options are outlined below. If you agree with one of the statements, you should initial that statement. Read all of these statements carefully before you initial your selection. You can also write your own statement concerning life-sustaining treatment and other matters relating to your health care. You may initial any combination of paragraphs 1, 2, 3 and 4 but if you initial paragraph 5, the other paragraphs should not be initialed.

[   ] 1. If I have a terminal condition I do not want my life to be prolonged and I do not want life-sustaining treatment, beyond comfort care, that would serve only to artificially delay the moment of my death.

[   ] 2. If I am in a terminal condition or an irreversible coma or a persistent vegetative state that my doctors reasonably feel to be irreversible or incurable, I do want the medical treatment necessary to provide care that would keep me comfortable, but I do not want the following:
[   ] (a) Cardiopulmonary resuscitation, for example, the use of drugs, electric shock and artificial breathing.
[   ] (b) Artificially administered food and fluids.
[   ] (c) To be taken to a hospital if at all avoidable.

[   ] 3. Notwithstanding my other directions, if I am known to be pregnant, I do not want life-sustaining treatment withheld or withdrawn if it is possible that the embryo/fetus will develop to the point of live birth with the continued application of life-sustaining treatment.

[   ] 4. Notwithstanding my other directions I do want the use of all medical care necessary to treat my condition until my doctors reasonably conclude that my condition is terminal or is irreversible and incurable or I am in a persistent vegetative state.

[   ] 5. I want my life to be prolonged to the greatest extent possible.

Other or Additional Statements of Desires: (initial your choice.)

I have [   ] OR I have not [   ] attached additional special provisions or limitations to this document to be honored in the absence of my being able to give health care directions.

Signature of Principal _____

Printed Name _____

Date _____

The above signature must be witnessed or acknowledged. Witness or Acknowledgement Form on reverse side if used.

I affirm that this was signed or acknowledged in my presence, and that the person signing this document (the principal) appears to be of sound mind and under no duress. I am not designated to make medical decisions on the principal's behalf. I am not directly involved with the provision of health care to the principal. I am not entitled to any portion of the principal's estate upon his or her decease, whether under any will or by operation of law. I am not related to the principal by blood, marriage, or adoption.

Witness Signature _____

Printed Name _____

Address _____

Witness Signature _____

Printed Name _____

Address _____

OR

State of _____
County of _____

On this date _____, before me, personally appeared _____, personally known to me (or proved to me on the basis of satisfactory evidence) to be the person whose name is subscribed to this instrument, and acknowledged that he or she executed it. I declare under penalty of perjury that the person whose name is subscribed to this instrument appears to be of sound mind and under no duress, fraud, or undue influence.

Notary Signature:_____   Notary Seal

Arkansas Living Will

If I should have an incurable or irreversible condition that will cause my death within a relatively short time, and I am no longer able to make decisions regarding my medical treatment OR if I should become permanently unconscious, I direct my attending physician, pursuant to the Arkansas Rights of the Terminally Ill or Permanently Unconscious Act, (initial your choice):

[   ] to withhold or withdraw treatment that only prolongs the process of dying and is not necessary to my comfort or to alleviate pain
Other directions:

I direct my attending physician, pursuant to the Arkansas Rights of the Terminally Ill or Permanently Unconscious Act, (initial your choice):

[   ] to follow the instructions of _____ whom I appoint as my Health Care Proxy to decide whether life-sustaining treatment should be withheld or withdrawn.

Signed this _____ day of_____, 20_____

Signature _____

Printed Name _____

Address_____

THE ABOVE SIGNATURE MUST BE WITNESSED BY TWO WITNESSES.

The declarant voluntarily signed this writing in my presence.

Witness _____

Printed Name _____

Address _____

Witness _____

Printed Name _____

Address _____

Pursuant to state law: A physician or other health care provider who is furnished a copy of the declaration shall make it a part of the declarant's medical record and, if unwilling to comply with the declaration, promptly so advise the declarant.

Colorado Living Will Declaration as to Medical or Surgical Treatment

I, _____(name of declarant), being of sound mind and at least eighteen years of age, direct that my life shall not be artificially prolonged under the circumstances set forth below and hereby declare that:

1. If at any time my attending physician and one other qualified physician certify in writing that:

a. I have an injury, disease, or illness which is not curable or reversible and which, in their judgment, is a terminal condition, and

b. For a period of seven consecutive days or more, I have been unconscious, comatose, or otherwise incompetent so as to be unable to make or communicate responsible decisions concerning my person, then:

I direct that, in accordance with Colorado law, life-sustaining procedures shall be withdrawn and withheld pursuant to the terms of this declaration, it being understood that life-sustaining procedures shall not include any medical procedure or intervention for nourishment considered necessary by the attending physician to provide comfort or alleviate pain. However, I may specifically direct, in accordance with Colorado law, that artificial nourishment be withdrawn or withheld pursuant to the terms of this declaration.

2. In the event that the only procedure I am being provided is artificial nourishment, I direct that one of the following actions be taken:

[   ] (initials of declarant) a. Artificial nourishment shall not be continued when it is the only procedure being provided; or

[   ] (initials of declarant) b. Artificial nourishment shall be continued for _____ days when it is the only procedure being provided; or

[   ] (initials of declarant) c. Artificial nourishment shall be continued when it is the only procedure being provided.

3. I execute this declaration, as my free and voluntary act, this _____ day of _____, 20___.

Signature _____
                             Declarant

The foregoing instrument was signed and declared by _____ to be his declaration, in the presence of us, who, in his presence, in the presence of each other, and at his request, have signed our names below as witnesses, and we declare that, at the time of the execution of this instrument, the declarant, according to our best knowledge and belief, was of sound mind and under no constraint or undue influence.

Dated at _____, Colorado, this _____ day of _____, 20___.

_____   _____   _____
           Signature   Printed name   Address

_____   _____   _____
           Signature   Printed name   Address

State of Colorado
County of _____

SUBSCRIBED and sworn to before me by _____, the declarant, and _____ and _____, the witnesses, as the voluntary act and deed of the declarant this _____ day of _____, 20___.

_____   My commission expires: _____
Notary Public Signature

Connecticut Living Will Health Care Instructions

To any physician who is treating me: These are my health care instructions including those concerning the withholding or withdrawal of life support systems,

I,_____, the author of this document, request that, if my condition is deemed terminal or if I am determined to be permanently unconscious, I be allowed to die and not be kept alive through life support systems.

By terminal condition, I mean that I have an incurable or irreversible medical condition which, without the administration of life support systems, will, in the opinion of my attending physician, result in death within a relatively short time.

By permanently unconscious I mean that I am in a permanent coma or persistent vegetative state which is an irreversible condition in which I am at no time aware of myself or the environment and show no behavioral response to the environment.

The life support systems which I do not want include, but are not limited to: Artificial respiration, cardio-pulmonary resuscitation and artificial means of providing nutrition and hydration.

I do want sufficient pain medication to maintain my physical comfort. I do not intend any direct taking of my life, but only that my dying not be unreasonably prolonged.

These requests, appointments, and designations are made after careful reflection, while I am of sound mind. Any party receiving a duly executed copy or facsimile of this document may rely upon it unless such party has received actual notice of my revocation of it.

Date _____, 20____.

_____
Signature of Author of Document

_____
Printed Name of Author of Document

State of Connecticut
County of _____

We, the subscribing witnesses, being duly sworn, say that we witnessed the execution of these health care instructions, that the author subscribed, published and declared the same to be the author's instructions, appointments and designation in our presence; that we thereafter subscribed the document as witnesses in the author's presence, at the author's request, and in the presence of each other; that at the time of the execution of said document the author appeared to us to be eighteen years of age or older, of sound mind, able to understand the nature and consequences of said document, and under no improper influence, and we make this affidavit at the author's request this _____ day of _____20____

_____
(Witness)

_____
(Witness Printed Name)

_____
(Witness)

_____
(Witness Printed Name)

Subscribed and sworn to before me this _____ day of _____20____

_____
Commissioner of the Superior Court
Notary Public   My commission expires:_____

Delaware Living Will Instructions For Health Care

If you fill out this form, you may strike any wording you do not want.

End-of-life Decisions: If I am in a qualifying condition, I direct that my health-care providers and others involved in my care provide, withhold, or withdraw treatment in accordance with the choices I have marked below:

Choice Not To Prolong Life. I do not want my life to be prolonged if: (please initial all that apply)
[   ] I have a terminal condition (an incurable condition caused by injury, disease, or illness which, to a reasonable degree of medical certainty, makes death imminent and from which, despite the application of life-sustaining procedures, there can be no recovery). Regarding artificial nutrition and hydration in this situation, I make the following specific directions: (Please initial your choices)
Artificial nutrition through a conduit (tube): [   ] yes, I want it used, OR
                                              [   ] no, I do not want it used
Hydration through a conduit (tube):   [   ] yes, I want it used, OR
                                              [   ] no, I do not want it used

[   ] I become permanently unconscious (a medical condition that has been diagnosed in accordance with currently accepted medical standards that has lasted at least 4 weeks and with reasonable medical certainty as total and irreversible loss of consciousness and capacity for interaction with the environment. The term includes, without limitation, a persistent vegetative state or irreversible coma. Regarding artificial nutrition and hydration in this situation, I make the following specific directions: (please initial your choices)
Artificial nutrition through a conduit (tube): [   ] yes, I want it used, OR
                                              [   ] no, I do not want it used
Hydration through a conduit (tube):   [   ] yes, I want it used, OR
                                              [   ] no, I do not want it used

Choice To Prolong Life (please initial if you choose)
[   ] I want my life to be prolonged as long as possible within the limits of generally accepted health-care standards.

Relief From Pain: Except as I state in the following space, I direct treatment for alleviation of pain or discomfort be provided at all times, even if it hastens my death:

Other Medical Instructions: (If you do not agree with any of the optional choices above and wish to write your own, or if you wish to add to the instructions you have given above, you may do so here.) I direct that: (Add additional sheets if necessary.)

Effect of Copy: A copy of this form has the same effect as the original.

Signature: Sign and date the form here: I understand the purpose and effect of this document.

_____

Date

_____

(address)

_____

Your Signature (Declarant)

_____

(print your name)

Witness statements and signatures required on reverse side

Signatures and Statements of Witnesses: Signed and Declared by the above-named declarant as and for his/her written declaration under 16 Del. C. §§ 2502 and 2503, in our presence, who in his/her presence, at his/her request, and in the presence of each other, have hereunto subscribed our names as witnesses, and state:

A. That the Declarant is mentally competent.
B. That neither of the witnesses:

      1. Is related to the declarant by blood, marriage or adoption;

      2. Is entitled to any portion of the estate of the declarant under any will of the declarant or codicil thereto then existing nor, at the time of the executing of the advance health care directive, is so entitled by operation of law then existing;

      3. Has, at the time of the execution of the advance health-care directive, a present or inchoate claim against any portion of the estate of the declarant;

      4. Has a direct financial responsibility for the declarant's medical care;

      5. Has a controlling interest in or is an operator or an employee of a residential long-term health-care institution in which the declarant is a resident; or

      6. Is under eighteen years of age.

C. That if the declarant is a resident of a sanitarium, rest home, nursing home, boarding home or related institution, one of the witnesses, _____, is at the time of the execution of the advance health-care directive, a patient advocate or ombudsman designated by the Division of Services for Aging and Adults with Physical Disabilities or the Public Guardian.

First witness

Date of Signature _____

_____
Signature of Witness

_____
Printed name of Witness

_____
Address of Witness

Second witness

Date of Signature _____

_____
Signature of Witness

_____
Printed name of Witness

_____
Address of Witness

District of Columbia (Washington D.C.) Living Will Declaration

Declaration made this date: _____

I, _____,
                                      (name)

being of sound mind, willfully and voluntarily make known my desires that my dying shall not be artificially prolonged under the circumstances set forth below, do declare:

If at any time I should have an incurable injury, disease or illness certified to be a terminal condition by two physicians who have personally examined me, one of whom shall be my attending physician, and the physicians have determined that my death will occur whether or not life-sustaining procedures are utilized and where the application of life-sustaining procedures would serve only to artificially prolong the dying process, I direct that such procedures be withheld or withdrawn, and that I be permitted to die naturally with only the administration of medication or the performance of any medical procedure deemed necessary to provide me with comfort care or to alleviate pain.

Other directions:

In the absence of my ability to give directions regarding the use of such life-sustaining procedures, it is my intention that this declaration shall be honored by my family and physician(s) as the final expression of my legal right to refuse medical or surgical treatment and accept the consequences from such refusal.

I understand the full import of this declaration and I am emotionally and mentally competent to make this declaration.

Signed _____

Address _____

I believe the declarant to be of sound mind. I did not sign the declarant's signature above for or at the direction of the declarant. I am at least eighteen years of age and am not related to the declarant by blood or marriage, entitled to any portion of the estate of the declarant according to the laws of intestate succession of the District of Columbia or under any will of the declarant or codicil thereto, or directly financially responsible for declarant's medical care. I am not the declarant's attending physician, an employee of the attending physician, or an employee of the health facility in which the declarant is a patient.

Witness #1 Signature _____

Printed Name _____

Witness #2 _____

Printed Name _____

Florida Living Will

Declaration made this _____ day of _____, 20___ , I, _____, willfully and voluntarily make known my desire that my dying not be artificially prolonged under the circumstances set forth below, and I do hereby declare that, if at any time I am incapacitated and *(initial each option desired--you may initial more than one.)*

[   ] I have a terminal condition, or

[   ] I have an end-stage condition, or

[   ] I am in a persistent vegetative state

and if my attending or treating physician and another consulting physician have determined that there is no reasonable medical probability of my recovery from such condition, I direct that life-prolonging procedures be withheld or withdrawn when the application of such procedures would serve only to prolong artificially the process of dying, and that I be permitted to die naturally with only the administration of medication or the performance of any medical procedure deemed necessary to provide me with comfort care or to alleviate pain.

It is my intention that this declaration be honored by my family and physician as the final expression of my legal right to refuse medical or surgical treatment and to accept the consequences for such refusal.

I understand the full import of this declaration, and I am emotionally and mentally competent to make this declaration.

Signature_____

Printed Name _____

This document must be witnessed by two (2) witnesses.

Witness #1 _____

Printed Name _____

Address _____

Witness #2_____

Printed Name _____

Address _____

Georgia Living Will

Living Will made this date: _____

I, _____,

(name)

being of sound mind, willfully and voluntarily make known my desire that my life shall not be prolonged under the circumstances set forth below and do declare:

1. If at any time I should: (initial each option desired):

[   ] have a terminal condition,

[   ] become in a coma with no reasonable expectation of regaining consciousness, or

[   ] become in a persistent vegetative state with no reasonable expectation of regaining significant cognitive function, as defined in and established in accordance with the procedures set forth in paragraphs (2), (9), and (13) of Code Section 31-32-2 of the Official Code of Georgia Annotated, I direct that the application of life-sustaining procedures to my body be withheld or withdrawn and that I be permitted to die.

With regard to artificially supplied nutrition and hydration, I direct that: (initial the option desired):

[   ] artificial nutrition be provided.

[   ] artificial nutrition be withheld or withdrawn.

(initial the option desired):

[   ] artificial hydration be provided.

[   ] artificial hydration be withheld or withdrawn.

Other directions:

2. In the absence of my ability to give directions regarding the use of such life-sustaining procedures, it is my intention that this living will shall be honored by my family and physician(s) as the final expression of my legal right to refuse medical or surgical treatment and accept the consequences from such refusal.

3. I understand that I may revoke this living will at any time.

4. I understand the full import of this living will, and I am at least 18 years of age and am emotionally and mentally competent to make this living will.

5. If I am a female and I have been diagnosed as pregnant, I want this living will to be carried out despite my pregnancy. [   ] (initial)

Signed _____

City _____

County _____

State of Residence _____

Witness Statement

I hereby witness this living will and attest that:

(1) The declarant is personally known to me and I believe the declarant to be at least 18 years of age and of sound mind;

(2) I am at least 18 years of age;

(3) To the best of my knowledge, at the time of the execution of this living will, I:

    (A) Am not related to the declarant by blood or marriage;

    (B) Would not be entitled to any portion of the declarant's estate by any will or by operation of law under the rules of descent and distribution of this state;

(C) Am not the attending physician of declarant or an employee of the attending physician or an employee of the hospital or skilled nursing facility in which declarant is a patient;

(D) Am not directly financially responsible for the declarant's medical care; and

(E) Have no present claim against any portion of the estate of the declarant;

(4) Declarant has signed this document in my presence as above instructed, on the date above first shown.

Witness #1 _____

Printed Name _____

Address _____

Witness #2 _____

Printed Name _____

Address _____

An additional witness is required when living will is signed by a patient in a hospital or skilled nursing facility. I hereby witness this living will and attest that I believe the declarant to be of sound mind and to have made this living will willingly and voluntarily.

Witness #3 _____

Printed Name _____

(Medical director of skilled nursing facility or staff physician not participating in care of the patient, or chief of the hospital medical staff or staff physician or hospital designee not participating in care of the patient.)

Hawaii Living Will and Instructions for Health Care

You have the right to give instructions about your own health care. This form allows you to do this. If you use this form, you may complete or modify all or any part of it. You are free to use a different form. This form lets you give specific instructions about any aspect of your health care, whether or not you appoint an agent. Choices are provided for you to express your wishes regarding the provision, withholding, or withdrawal of treatment to keep you alive, as well as the provision of pain relief. Space is provided for you to add to the choices you have made or for you to write out any additional wishes. You have the right to revoke this advance health care directive or replace this form at any time. If you fill out this part of the form, you may strike any wording you do not want.

End-of-life Decisions: I direct that my health care providers and others involved in my care provide, withhold, or withdraw treatment in accordance with the choice I have marked below: (Initial only one box)

[   ] **Choice NOT To Prolong Life**. I do not want my life to be prolonged if (1) I have an incurable and irreversible condition that will result in my death within a relatively short time, (2) I become unconscious and, to a reasonable degree of medical certainty, I will not regain consciousness, or (3) the likely risks and burdens of treatment would outweigh the expected benefits,

OR

[   ] **Choice To Prolong Life**. I want my life to be prolonged as long as possible within the limits of generally accepted health care standards.

Relief From Pain: Except as I state in the following space, I direct that treatment for alleviation of pain or discomfort should be provided at all times even if it hastens my death:

Other Wishes: (If you do not agree with any of the optional choices above and wish to write your own, or if you wish to add to the instructions you have given above, you may do so here.) I direct that: (Add additional sheets if needed.)

Effect of Copy: A copy of this form has the same effect as the original.

Signature: Sign and date the form here:
Date:_____

Signature:_____
Printed Name:_____
Address:_____

Witnesses: This advance health care directive will not be valid for making health care decisions unless it is either:
(A) signed by two (2) qualified adult witnesses who are personally known to you and who are present when you sign or acknowledge your signature; OR
(B) acknowledged before a notary public.

Alternative (A): Signed by Witnesses
Witness #1 Statement:
I declare under penalty of perjury under the laws of Hawaii (1) that the individual who signed or acknowledged this advance health care directive is personally known to me, or that the individual's identity was proven to me by convincing evidence, (2) that the individual signed or acknowledged this advance directive in my presence, (3) that the individual appears to be of sound mind and under no duress, fraud or undue influence, (4) that I am not a

person appointed as an agent by this advance directive, and (5) that I am not the individual's health care provider, an employee of the individual's health care provider, the operator of a community care facility, an employee of an operator of a community care facility, the operator of a residential care facility for the elderly, nor an employee of an operator of a residential care facility for the elderly.

Date:_____

Witness #1 Signature:_____

Printed Name:_____

Address:_____

Witness #2 Statement:

I declare under penalty of perjury under the laws of Hawaii (1) that the individual who signed or acknowledged this advance health care directive is personally known to me, or that the individual's identity was proven to me by convincing evidence, (2) that the individual signed or acknowledged this advance directive in my presence, (3) that the individual appears to be of sound mind and under no duress, fraud or undue influence, (4) that I am not a person appointed as an agent by this advance directive, and (5) that I am not the individual's health care provider, an employee of the individual's health care provider, the operator of a community care facility, an employee of an operator of a community care facility, the operator of a residential care facility for the elderly, nor an employee of an operator of a residential care facility for the elderly. I further declare under penalty of perjury under the laws of Hawaii that I am not related to the individual executing this advance health care directive by blood, marriage, or adoption, and, to the best of my knowledge, I am not entitled to any part of the individual's estate upon his or her death under a will now existing or by operation of law.

Date:_____

Witness #2 Signature:_____

Printed Name:_____

Address:_____

Alternative (B): Acknowledged by Notary Public

State of Hawaii
County of _____
On this _____ day of _____, in the year _____, before me, personally appeared _____
_____, personally known to me (or proved to me on the basis of satisfactory evidence) to be the person whose name is subscribed to this instrument, and acknowledged that he or she executed it. I declare under penalty of perjury that the person whose name is subscribed to this instrument appears to be of sound mind and under no duress, fraud, or undue influence.

Notary Signature:_____   Notary Seal

Idaho Living Will Directive to Withhold or to Provide Treatment

To my family, my relatives, my friends, my physicians, my employers, and all others whom it may concern:
Directive made this _____ day of _____ 20___. I,_____ (name), being of sound mind, willfully, and voluntarily make known my desire that my life shall not be prolonged artificially under the circumstances set forth below, do hereby declare:

1. If at any time I should have an incurable injury, disease, illness or condition certified to be terminal by two medical doctors who have examined me, and where the application of life-sustaining procedures of any kind would serve only to prolong artificially the moment of my death, and where a medical doctor determines that my death is imminent, whether or not life-sustaining procedures are utilized, or I have been diagnosed as being in a persistent vegetative state, I direct that the following marked expression of my intent be followed and that I be permitted to die naturally, and that I receive any medical treatment or care that may be required to keep me free of pain or distress. (initial one)

[   ] If at any time I should become unable to communicate my instructions, then I direct that all medical treatment, care, and nutrition and hydration necessary to restore my health, sustain my life, and to abolish or alleviate pain or distress be provided to me. Nutrition and hydration shall not be withheld or withdrawn from me if I would die from malnutrition or dehydration rather than from my injury, disease, illness or condition.

[   ] If at any time I should become unable to communicate my instructions and where the application of artificial life-sustaining procedures shall serve only to prolong artificially the moment of my death, I direct such procedures be withheld or withdrawn except for the administration of nutrition and hydration.

[   ] If at any time I should become unable to communicate my instructions and where the application of artificial life-sustaining procedures shall serve only to prolong artificially the moment of death, I direct such procedures be withheld or withdrawn including withdrawal of the administration of nutrition and hydration.

2. In the absence of my ability to give directions regarding the use of life-sustaining procedures, I hereby appoint _____(name) currently residing at _____, as my attorney-in-fact/proxy for the making of decisions relating to my health care in my place; and it is my intention that this appointment shall be honored by him/her, by my family, relatives, friends, physicians and lawyer as the final expression of my legal right to refuse medical or surgical treatment; and I accept the consequences of such a decision. I have duly executed a Durable Power of Attorney for health care decisions on this date.

3. In the absence of my ability to give further directions regarding my treatment, including life-sustaining procedures, it is my intention that this directive shall be honored by my family and physicians as the final expression of my legal right to refuse or accept medical and surgical treatment, and I accept the consequences of such refusal.

4. If I have been diagnosed as pregnant and that diagnosis is known to any interested person, this directive shall have no force during the course of my pregnancy.

5. I understand the full importance of this directive and am emotionally and mentally competent to make this directive. No participant in the making of this directive or in its being carried into effect, whether it be a medical doctor, my spouse, a relative, friend or any other person shall be held responsible in any way, legally, professionally or socially, for complying with my directions.

Signed_____   **Witness signatures on reverse side**

_____
City, county and state of residence

The declarant has been known to me personally and I believe him/her to be of sound mind.

Witness #1 _____

Printed Name _____

Address _____

Witness #2 _____

Printed Name _____

Address _____

Illinois Living Will Declaration

This declaration is made this _____ day of _____, 20____.

I, _____, being of sound mind, willfully and voluntarily make known my desires that my moment of death shall not be artificially postponed.

If at any time I should have an incurable and irreversible injury, disease, or illness judged to be a terminal condition by my attending physician who has personally examined me and has determined that my death is imminent except for death delaying procedures, then

I direct that such procedures which would only prolong the dying process be withheld or withdrawn, and that I be permitted to die naturally with only the administration of medication, sustenance, or the performance of any medical procedure deemed necessary by my attending physician to provide me with comfort care.

In the absence of my ability to give directions regarding the use of such death delaying procedures, it is my intention that this declaration shall be honored by my family and physician as the final expression of my legal right to refuse medical or surgical treatment and accept the consequences from such refusal.

Signed_____

_____

City, County and State of Residence

The declarant is personally known to me and I believe him or her to be of sound mind. I saw the declarant sign the declaration in my presence (or the declarant acknowledged in my presence that he or she had signed the declaration) and I signed the declaration as a witness in the presence of the declarant. I did not sign the declarant's signature above for or at the direction of the declarant. At the date of this instrument, I am not entitled to any portion of the estate of the declarant according to the laws of intestate succession or, to the best of my knowledge and belief, under any will of declarant or other instrument taking effect at declarant's death, or directly financially responsible for declarant's medical care.

Witness #1 _____

Printed Name _____

Witness #2 _____

Printed Name _____

Indiana Living Will Declaration

Declaration made this _____ day of _____, 20___. I, _____, being at least eighteen (18) years of age and of sound mind, willfully and voluntarily make known my desires that my dying shall not be artificially prolonged under the circumstances set forth below, and I declare:

If at any time my attending physician certifies in writing that:
1) I have an incurable injury, disease, or illness; and
(2) my death will occur within a short time; and
(3) the use of life prolonging procedures would serve only to artificially prolong the dying process, then

I direct that such procedures be withheld or withdrawn, and that I be permitted to die naturally with only the performance or provision of any medical procedure or medication necessary to provide me with comfort care or to alleviate pain, and, if I have so indicated below, the provision of artificially supplied nutrition and hydration. (Indicate your choice by initialing or making your mark before signing this declaration):

[   ] I wish to receive artificially supplied nutrition and hydration, even if the effort to sustain life is futile or excessively burdensome to me.

[   ] I do not wish to receive artificially supplied nutrition and hydration, if the effort to sustain life is futile or excessively burdensome to me.

[   ] I intentionally make no decision concerning artificially supplied nutrition and hydration, leaving the decision to my health care representative appointed under IC 16-36-1-7 or my attorney in fact with health care powers under IC 30-5-5.

In the absence of my ability to give directions regarding the use of life prolonging procedures, it is my intention that this declaration be honored by my family and physician as the final expression of my legal right to refuse medical or surgical treatment and accept the consequences of the refusal.

I understand the full import of this declaration.

Signed _____

_____
City, County, and State of Residence

The declarant has been personally known to me, and I believe (him/her) to be of sound mind. I did not sign the declarant's signature above for or at the direction of the declarant. I am not a parent, spouse, or child of the declarant. I am not entitled to any part of the declarant's estate or directly financially responsible for the declarant's medical care. I am competent and at least eighteen (18) years of age.

Witness #1 _____ Date _____

Printed Name _____

Witness #2 _____ Date _____

Printed Name _____

Iowa Living Will Declaration

If I should have an incurable or irreversible condition that will result either in death within a relatively short period of time or a state of permanent unconsciousness from which, to a reasonable degree of medical certainty, there can be no recovery, it is my desire that my life not be prolonged by the administration of life-sustaining procedures. If I am unable to participate in my health care decisions, I direct my attending physician to withhold or withdraw life-sustaining procedures that merely prolong the dying process and are not necessary to my comfort or freedom from pain.

I, the principal, sign my name to this instrument this _____ day of _____, 20 _____, and being first duly sworn, do hereby declare to the undersigned that I am eighteen years of age or older, of sound mind, and under no undue constraint or influence.

_____
Principal signature

_____
Principal Printed Name

This Document Must Either Be Witnessed by Two (2) Witnesses OR by a Notary Public

Witness Statements
Witness #1
I declare that the person who signed or acknowledged this document is personally known to me, that he/she signed or acknowledged this durable power of attorney in my presence, and that he/she appears to be of sound mind and under no duress, fraud or undue influence. I am not the person designated as attorney in fact by this document, nor am I the principal's health care provider or an employee of the principal's health care provider. I am at least eighteen years of age.

Signature _____ Date _____

Print Name _____

Address _____

Witness #2
I declare that the person who signed or acknowledged this document is personally known to me, that he/she signed or acknowledged this durable power of attorney in my presence, and that he/she appears to be of sound mind and under no duress, fraud or undue influence. I am not the person designated as attorney in fact by this document, nor am I the principal's health care provider or an employee of the principal's health care provider. I am at least eighteen years of age. I further declare that I am not a relative of the principal by blood, marriage or adoption (within the third degree of consanguinity).

Signature _____ Date _____

Print Name _____

Address _____

OR Notary Public Acknowledgement on reverse side

The State of Iowa
The County of _____

Signed and sworn to before me by _____,
the principal, this _____ day of _____, 20_____.

(SEAL) _____
                    (notary public)

Kansas Living Will Declaration

Living Will and Declaration made this date: _____.

I, _____,
                             (name)

being of sound mind, willfully and voluntarily make known my desire that my dying shall not be artificially prolonged under the circumstances set forth below, and do hereby declare:

If at any time I should have an incurable injury, disease, or illness certified to be a terminal condition by two physicians who have personally examined me, one of whom shall be my attending physician, and the physicians have determined that my death will occur whether or not life-sustaining procedures are utilized and where the application of life-sustaining procedures would serve only to artificially prolong the dying process, then

I direct that such procedures be withheld or withdrawn, and that I be permitted to die naturally with only the administration of medication or the performance of any medical procedure deemed necessary to provide me with comfort care.

In the absence of my ability to give directions regarding the use of such life-sustaining procedures, it is my intention that this declaration shall be honored by my family and physician(s) as the final expression of my legal right to refuse medical or surgical treatment and accept the consequences from such refusal. I understand the full import of this declaration and I am emotionally and mentally competent to make this declaration.
Other directions:

Executed this _____ day of _____ ,20____ , at _____ , Kansas.

_____
                  Signature of Principal

This document must be: (1) Witnessed by two individuals of lawful age who are not the agent, not related to the principal by blood, marriage or adoption, not entitled to any portion of principal's estate and not financially responsible for principal's health care; OR (2) acknowledged by a notary public (on reverse side of form).

Witness #1 Signature _____

Printed Name _____

Address _____

Witness #2 Signature _____

Printed Name _____

Address _____

Or Notary Acknowledgement on reverse

State of _____

County of _____

This instrument was acknowledged before me on _____(date)
by_____ (name of principal).

_____ (Signature of notary public)

(Seal, if any)   My appointment expires:_____

Kentucky Living Will Advance Directive

My wishes regarding life-prolonging treatment and artificially provided nutrition and hydration to be provided to me if I no longer have decisional capacity, have a terminal condition, or become permanently unconscious have been indicated by checking and initialing the appropriate lines below. By checking and initialing the appropriate lines, I specifically:

The following are my directions to my attending physician. If I have designated a health care surrogate, my surrogate shall comply with my wishes as indicated below:

(Initial One)
[   ] Direct that treatment be withheld or withdrawn, and that I be permitted to die naturally with only the administration of medication or the performance of any medical treatment deemed necessary to alleviate pain.
[   ] DO NOT authorize that life-prolonging treatment be withheld or withdrawn.

(Initial One)
[   ] Authorize the withholding or withdrawal of artificially provided food, water, or other artificially provided nourishment or fluids.
[   ] DO NOT authorize the withholding or withdrawal of artificially provided food, water, or other artificially provided nourishment or fluids.
[   ] Authorize my surrogate, designated above, to withhold or withdraw artificially provided nourishment or fluids, or other treatment if the surrogate determines that withholding or withdrawing is in my best interest; but I do not mandate that withholding or withdrawing.

(Initial One)
[   ] Authorize the giving of all or any part of my body upon death for any purpose specified in KRS 311.185.
[   ] DO NOT authorize the giving of all or any part of my body upon death.

In the absence of my ability to give directions regarding the use of life-prolonging treatment and artificially provided nutrition and hydration, it is my intention that this directive shall be honored by my attending physician, my family, and any health care surrogate that I have designated as the final expression of my legal right to refuse medical or surgical treatment and I accept the consequences of the refusal.

If I have been diagnosed as pregnant and that diagnosis is known to my attending physician, this directive shall have no force or effect during the course of my pregnancy.

I understand the full import of this directive and I am emotionally and mentally competent to make this directive.
Signed this _____ day of _____, 20____.

Signature_____

Printed Name_____

_____
Address

This document must be witnessed by two (2) witnesses
OR acknowledged by a Notary Public on the reverse side.

In our joint presence, the grantor, who is of sound mind and eighteen (18) years of age, or older, voluntarily dated and signed this writing or directed it to be dated and signed for the grantor.

Witness #1 Signature _____

Printed Name _____

Address _____

Witness #2 Signature _____

Printed Name _____

Address _____

OR

STATE OF KENTUCKY
_____County

Before me, the undersigned authority, came _____ who is of sound mind and eighteen (18) years of age, or older, and acknowledged that he voluntarily dated and signed this writing or directed it to be signed and dated as above.

Done this _____ day of_____, 20____.

_____
Signature of Notary Public or other officer

Date commission expires_____

Louisiana Living Will Declaration

Declaration made this _____ day of _____,20____ .

I, _____, being of sound mind, willfully and voluntarily make known my desire that my dying shall not be artificially prolonged under the circumstances set forth below and do hereby declare:

If at any time I should have an incurable injury, disease or illness, or be in a continual profound comatose state with no reasonable chance of recovery, certified to be a terminal and irreversible condition by two physicians who have personally examined me, one of whom shall be my attending physician, and the physicians have determined that my death will occur whether or not life-sustaining procedures are utilized and where the application of life-sustaining procedure would serve only to prolong artificially the dying process, then

I direct that such procedures be withheld or withdrawn and that I be permitted to die naturally with only the administration of medication or the performance of any medical procedure deemed necessary to provide me with comfort care.

In the absence of my ability to give directions regarding the use of such life-sustaining procedures, it is my intention that this declaration shall be honored by my family and physician(s) as the final expression of my legal right to refuse medical or surgical treatment and accept the consequences from such refusal.

I understand the full import of this declaration and I am emotionally and mentally competent to make this declaration.

Signed _____

_____

City, Parish and State of Residence

This Declaration must be signed by two (2) witnesses.

The declarant has been personally known to me and I believe him or her to be of sound mind.

Witness #1 Signature _____

Printed Name _____

Address _____

Witness #2 Signature _____

Printed Name _____

Address _____

Maine Instructions for Health Care (Living Will)

If you do fill out this form, you may strike any wording you do not want.

End-of-life Decisions: I direct that my health-care providers and others involved in my care provide, withhold or withdraw treatment in accordance with the choice I have initialed below:

[   ] **Choice Not To Prolong Life:** I do not want my life to be prolonged if (i) I have an incurable and irreversible condition that will result in my death within a relatively short time, (ii) I become unconscious and, to a reasonable degree of medical certainty, I will not regain consciousness, or (iii) the likely risks and burdens of treatment would outweigh the expected benefits.
OR
[   ] **Choice To Prolong Life:** I want my life to be prolonged as long as possible within the limits of generally accepted health-care standards.

Artificial Nutrition and Hydration: Artificial nutrition and hydration must be provided, withheld or withdrawn in accordance with the choice I have made above, unless I mark the following box. If I initial this box [ ], artificial nutrition and hydration must be provided regardless of my condition and regardless of the choice I have made above.

Relief from Pain: Except as I state in the following space, I direct that treatment for alleviation of pain or discomfort be provided at all times, even if it hastens my death:

Other Wishes: (If you do not agree with any of the optional choices above and wish to write your own, or if you wish to add to the instructions you have given above, you may do so here.) I direct that: (Add additional sheets if needed)

Effect of Copy: A copy of this form has the same effect as the original.

Signature: Sign and date the form here:

_____   _____
(date)   (sign your name)

_____   _____
(address)   (print your name)

_____
(city)   (state)

Signatures of Witnesses:

Signature of first witness _____date_____
First witness printed name _____

_____
First witness address

Signature of second witness _____date_____
Second witness printed name _____

_____
Second witness address

Maryland Living Will Advance Health Care Directive

If I am not able to make an informed decision regarding my health care, I direct my health care providers to follow my instructions as set forth below. (Initial those statements you wish to be included in the document and cross through those statements which do not apply.)

(a). If my death from a terminal condition is imminent and even if life-sustaining procedures are used there is no reasonable expectation of my recovery (initial one)

[   ] I direct that my life not be extended by life-sustaining procedures, including the administration of nutrition and hydration artificially.

[   ] I direct that my life not be extended by life-sustaining procedures, except that, if I am unable to take food by mouth, I wish to receive nutrition and hydration artificially.

[   ] I direct that, even in a terminal condition, I be given all available medical treatment in accordance with accepted health care standards.

(b). If I am in a persistent vegetative state, that is if I am not conscious and am not aware of my environment nor able to interact with others, and there is no reasonable expectation of my recovery within a medically appropriate period (initial one)

[   ] I direct that my life not be extended by life-sustaining procedures, including the administration of nutrition and hydration artificially.

[   ] I direct that my life not be extended by life-sustaining procedures, except that if I am unable to take in food by mouth, I wish to receive nutrition and hydration artificially.

[   ] I direct that I be given all available medical treatment in accordance with accepted health care standards.

c. If I am pregnant my agent shall follow these specific instructions:

By signing below, I indicate that I am emotionally and mentally competent to make this living will and that I understand its purpose and effect.

_____   _____
Date   Signature of Declarant

The declarant signed or acknowledged signing this living will in my presence and based upon my personal observation the declarant appears to be a competent individual.

_____date_____
Witness #1 Signature

Printed Name _____

_____date_____
Witness #2 Signature

Printed Name_____

Massachusetts Living Will Declaration And Directive to Physicians

I,_____ , willfully and voluntarily make known my desire that my life not be artificially prolonged under the circumstances set forth below, and, pursuant to any and all applicable laws in the State of Massachusetts , I declare that:

1. If at any time I should have an incurable injury, disease, or illness which has been certified as a terminal condition by my attending physician and one additional physician, both of whom have personally examined me, and such physicians have determined that there can be no recovery from such condition and my death is imminent, and where the application of life-prolonging procedures would serve only to artificially prolong the dying process, I direct that such procedures be withheld or withdrawn, and that I be permitted to die naturally with only the administration of medication, the administration of nutrition, or the performance of any medical procedure deemed necessary to provide me with comfort, care, or to alleviate pain.

2. If at any time I should have been diagnosed as being in a persistent vegetative state which has been certified as incurable by my attending physician and one additional physician, both of whom have personally examined me, and such physicians have determined that there can be no recovery from such condition, and where the application of life-prolonging procedures would serve only to artificially prolong the dying process, I direct that such procedures be withheld or withdrawn, and that I be permitted to die naturally with only the administration of medication, the administration of nutrition, or the performance of any medical procedure deemed necessary to provide me with comfort, care, or to alleviate pain.

3. In the absence of my ability to give directions regarding my treatment in the above situations, including directions regarding the use of such life-prolonging procedures, it is my intention that this declaration shall be honored by my family, my physician, and any court of law, as the final expression of my legal right to refuse medical and surgical treatment. I declare that I fully accept the consequences for such refusal.

4. If I am diagnosed as pregnant, this document shall have no force and effect during my pregnancy.

5. I understand the full importance of this declaration, and I am emotionally and mentally competent to make this declaration and Living Will. No person shall be in any way responsible for the making or placing into effect of this declaration and Living Will or for carrying out my express directions. I also understand that I may revoke this document at any time.

I publish and sign this Living Will and Directive to Physicians and declare that I do so freely, for the purposes expressed, under no constraint or undue influence, and that I am of sound mind and of legal age.

_____
Declarant's Signature

_____
Printed Name of Declarant

Witness Statements
On _____ , in the presence of all of us, the above-named Declarant published and signed this Living Will and Directive to Physicians, and then at the Declarant's request, and in the Declarant's presence, and in each other's presence, we all signed below as witnesses, and we each declare, under penalty of perjury, that, to the best of our knowledge:

1. The Declarant is personally known to me and, to the best of my knowledge, the Declarant signed this instrument freely, under no constraint or undue influence, and is of sound mind and memory and legal age, and fully aware

of the possible consequences of this action.

2. I am at least 19 (nineteen) years of age and I am not related to the Declarant in any manner by blood, marriage, or adoption.

3. I am not the Declarant's attending physician, or a patient or employee of the Declarant's attending physician, or a patient, physician, or employee of the health care facility in which the Declarant is a patient, unless such person is required or allowed to witness the execution of this document by the laws of the state in which this document is executed.

4. I am not entitled to any portion of the Declarant's estate on the Declarant's death under the laws of intestate succession of any state or country, nor under the Last Will and Testament of the Declarant or any Codicil to such Last Will and Testament.

5. I have no claim against any portion of the Declarant's estate on the Declarant's death.

6. I am not directly financially responsible for the Declarant's medical care.

7. I did not sign the Declarant's signature for the Declarant or on the direction of the Declarant, nor have I been paid any fee for acting as a witness to the execution of this document.

_____   _____
Signature of Witness #1   Date

_____
Printed Name of Witness

_____
Address of Witness

_____   _____
Signature of Witness #2   Date

_____
Printed Name of Witness

_____
Address of Witness

Michigan Living Will Declaration and Directive to Physicians

I,_____ , willfully and voluntarily make known my desire that my life not be artificially prolonged under the circumstances set forth below, and, pursuant to any and all applicable laws in the State of Michigan, I declare that:

1. If at any time I should have an incurable injury, disease, or illness which has been certified as a terminal condition by my attending physician and one additional physician, both of whom have personally examined me, and such physicians have determined that there can be no recovery from such condition and my death is imminent, and where the application of life-prolonging procedures would serve only to artificially prolong the dying process, I direct that such procedures be withheld or withdrawn, and that I be permitted to die naturally with only the administration of medication, the administration of nutrition, or the performance of any medical procedure deemed necessary to provide me with comfort, care, or to alleviate pain.

2. If at any time I should have been diagnosed as being in a persistent vegetative state which has been certified as incurable by my attending physician and one additional physician, both of whom have personally examined me, and such physicians have determined that there can be no recovery from such condition, and where the application of life-prolonging procedures would serve only to artificially prolong the dying process, I direct that such procedures be withheld or withdrawn, and that I be permitted to die naturally with only the administration of medication, the administration of nutrition, or the performance of any medical procedure deemed necessary to provide me with comfort, care, or to alleviate pain.

3. In the absence of my ability to give directions regarding my treatment in the above situations, including directions regarding the use of such life-prolonging procedures, it is my intention that this declaration shall be honored by my family, my physician, and any court of law, as the final expression of my legal right to refuse medical and surgical treatment. I declare that I fully accept the consequences for such refusal.

4. If I am diagnosed as pregnant, this document shall have no force and effect during my pregnancy.

5. I understand the full importance of this declaration, and I am emotionally and mentally competent to make this declaration and Living Will. No person shall be in any way responsible for the making or placing into effect of this declaration and Living Will or for carrying out my express directions. I also understand that I may revoke this document at any time.

I publish and sign this Living Will and Directive to Physicians and declare that I do so freely, for the purposes expressed, under no constraint or undue influence, and that I am of sound mind and of legal age.

_____

Declarant's Signature

_____

Printed Name of Declarant

Witness Statements

On _____ , in the presence of all of us, the above-named Declarant published and signed this Living Will and Directive to Physicians, and then at the Declarant's request, and in the Declarant's presence, and in each other's presence, we all signed below as witnesses, and we each declare, under penalty of perjury, that, to the best of our knowledge:

1. The Declarant is personally known to me and, to the best of my knowledge, the Declarant signed this instrument freely, under no constraint or undue influence, and is of sound mind and memory and legal age, and fully aware

of the possible consequences of this action.

2. I am at least 19 (nineteen) years of age and I am not related to the Declarant in any manner by blood, marriage, or adoption.

3. I am not the Declarant's attending physician, or a patient or employee of the Declarant's attending physician, or a patient, physician, or employee of the health care facility in which the Declarant is a patient, unless such person is required or allowed to witness the execution of this document by the laws of the state in which this document is executed.

4. I am not entitled to any portion of the Declarant's estate on the Declarant's death under the laws of intestate succession of any state or country, nor under the Last Will and Testament of the Declarant or any Codicil to such Last Will and Testament.

5. I have no claim against any portion of the Declarant's estate on the Declarant's death.

6. I am not directly financially responsible for the Declarant's medical care.

7. I did not sign the Declarant's signature for the Declarant or on the direction of the Declarant, nor have I been paid any fee for acting as a witness to the execution of this document.

_____   _____

Signature of Witness #1   Date

_____

Printed Name of Witness

_____

Address of Witness

_____   _____

Signature of Witness #2   Date

_____

Printed Name of Witness

_____

Address of Witness

Minnesota Living Will Health Care Instructions

To My Family, Doctors, And All Those Concerned With My Care:

I, _____, born on_____ (birth date), being an adult of sound mind, willfully and voluntarily make this statement as a directive to be followed if I am in a terminal condition and become unable to participate in decisions regarding my health care. I understand that my health care providers are legally bound to act consistently with my wishes, within the limits of reasonable medical practice and other applicable law. I also understand that I have the right to make medical and health care decisions for myself as long as I am able to do so and to revoke this living will at any time.

(1) The following are my feelings and wishes regarding my health care (you may state the circumstances under which this living will applies):

(2) I particularly want to have all appropriate health care that will help in the following ways (you may give instructions for care you do want):

(3) I particularly do not want the following (you may list specific treatment you do not want in certain circumstances):

(4) I particularly want to have the following kinds of life-sustaining treatment if I am diagnosed to have a terminal condition (you may list the specific types of life-sustaining treatment that you do want if you have a terminal condition):

(5) I particularly do not want the following kinds of life-sustaining treatment if I am diagnosed to have a terminal condition (you may list the specific types of life-sustaining treatment that you do not want if you have a terminal condition):

(6) I recognize that if I reject artificially administered sustenance, then I may die of dehydration or malnutrition rather than from my illness or injury. The following are my feelings and wishes regarding artificially administered sustenance should I have a terminal condition (you may indicate whether you wish to receive food and fluids given to you in some other way than by mouth if you have a terminal condition):

(7) Thoughts I feel are relevant to my instructions. (You may, but need not, give your religious beliefs, philosophy, or other personal values that you feel are important. You may also state preferences concerning the location of your care.)

DATE_____

SIGNED_____

This document must either be acknowledged before a Notary Public or witnesses by two (2) witnesses on the reverse side.

State of Minnesota

County Of_____

Subscribed, sworn to, and acknowledged before me by _____ on this _____

day of _____, 20____.

_____

Notary Public

OR

(Sign and date here in the presence of two adult witnesses, neither of whom is entitled to any part of your estate under a will or by operation of law, and neither of whom is your proxy.)

I certify that the declarant voluntarily signed this living will in my presence and that the declarant is personally known to me. I am not named as a proxy by the living will, and to the best of my knowledge, I am not entitled to any part of the estate of the declarant under a will or by operation of law.

Witness #1 Signature _____

Printed Name _____

Address _____

Witness #2 Signature _____

Printed Name _____

Address _____

Mississippi Living Will Advance Health Care Instructions

You have the right to give instructions about your own health care. This form lets you do this. If you use this form, you may complete or modify all or any part of it. You are free to use a different form. This form lets you give specific instructions about any aspect of your health care. Choices are provided for you to express your wishes regarding the provision, withholding, or withdrawal of treatment to keep you alive, including the provision of artificial nutrition and hydration, as well as the provision of pain relief. Space is provided for you to add to the choices you have made or for you to write out any additional wishes. You have the right to revoke this advance health-care directive or replace this form at any time.

End-of-life Decisions: I direct that my health-care providers and others involved in my care provide, withhold or withdraw treatment in accordance with the choice I have initialed below:

[   ] **Choice NOT To Prolong Life:** I do not want my life to be prolonged if (I) I have an incurable and irreversible condition that will result in my death within a relatively short time, (ii) I become unconscious and, to a reasonable degree of medical certainty, I will not regain consciousness, or (iii) the likely risks and burdens of treatment would outweigh the expected benefits,

OR

[   ] **Choice To Prolong Life:** I want my life to be prolonged as long as possible within the limits of generally accepted health-care standards.

Artificial Nutrition And Hydration: Artificial nutrition and hydration must be provided, withheld or withdrawn in accordance with the choice I have made above unless I initial the following box. If I initial this box [   ], artificial nutrition and hydration must be provided regardless of my condition and regardless of the choice I have made above.

Relief from Pain: Except as I state in the following space, I direct that treatment for alleviation of pain or discomfort be provided at all times, even if it hastens my death:

Other Wishes: (If you do not agree with any of the optional choices above and wish to write your own, or if you wish to add to the instructions you have given above, you may do so here.) I direct that: (Add additional sheets if needed.)

Effect of Copy: A copy of this form has the same effect as the original.

Signature: Sign and date the form here:

_____   _____
      (sign your name)   (date)

_____   _____
      (print your name)   (address)

_____   _____
      (city)   (state)

Witnesses: This Living Will will not be valid for health-care decisions unless it is either: (a) signed by two (2) qualified adult witnesses who are personally known to you and who are present when you sign or acknowledge your signature: or (b) acknowledged before a notary public in the state.
Witness signatures or Notary Acknowledgement on reverse side of document

Alternative (A)

Witness #1
I declare under penalty of perjury pursuant to Section 97-9-61, Mississippi Code of 1972, that the principal is personally known to me, that the principal signed or acknowledged this power of attorney in my presence, that the principal appears to be of sound mind and under no duress, fraud or undue influence, that I am not the person appointed as agent by this document, and that I am not a health-care provider, nor an employee of a health-care provider or facility. I am not related to the principal by blood, marriage or adoption, and to the best of my knowledge, I am not entitled to any part of the estate of the principal upon the death of the principal under a will now existing or by operation of law.

_____   _____
(Witness signature)   (date)

_____   _____
(Witness printed name)   (address)

_____   _____
(city)   (state)

Witness #2
I declare under penalty of perjury pursuant to Section 97-9-61, Mississippi Code of 1972, that the principal is personally known to me, that the principal signed or acknowledged this power of attorney in my presence, that the principal appears to be of sound mind and under no duress, fraud or undue influence, that I am not the person appointed as agent by this document, and that I am not a health-care provider, nor an employee of a health-care provider or facility.

_____   _____
(Witness signature)   (date)

_____   _____
(Witness printed name)   (address)

_____   _____
(city)   (state)

OR Alternative (B)

State of _____

County of _____

On this _____ day of _____, in the year _____, before me, a notary public, appeared _____, personally known to me (or proved to me on the basis of satisfactory evidence) to be the person whose name is subscribed to this instrument, and acknowledged that he or she executed it. I declare under the penalty of perjury that the person whose name is subscribed to this instrument appears to be of sound mind and under no duress, fraud or undue influence.

Notary Seal

_____
(Signature of Notary Public)

Missouri Living Will Declaration

I have the primary right to make my own decisions concerning treatment that might unduly prolong the dying process. By this declaration I express to my physician, family and friends my intent.

If I should have a terminal condition it is my desire that my dying not be prolonged by administration of death-prolonging procedures.

If my condition is terminal and I am unable to participate in decisions regarding my medical treatment, I direct my attending physician to withhold or withdraw medical procedures that merely prolong the dying process and are not necessary to my comfort or to alleviate pain.

It is not my intent to authorize affirmative or deliberate acts or omissions to shorten my life rather only to permit the natural process of dying.

Signed this _____ day of _____, 20_____

Signature_____

Printed Name _____

_____
City, County and State of residence

The declarant is known to me, is eighteen years of age or older, of sound mind and voluntarily signed this document in my presence.

Witness #1 Signature _____

Printed Name _____

Address _____

Witness #2 Signature _____

Printed Name _____

Address _____

Montana Living Will Declaration

If I should have an incurable or irreversible condition that, without the administration of life-sustaining treatment, will, in the opinion of my attending physician, cause my death within a relatively short time and I am no longer able to make decisions regarding my medical treatment, then

I direct my attending physician, pursuant to the Montana Rights of the Terminally Ill Act, to withhold or withdraw treatment that only prolongs the process of dying and is not necessary to my comfort or to alleviate pain.

Signed this _____ day of _____, 20____.

Signature_____

Printed Name _____

_____
City, County, and State of Residence

This document must be witnessed by two (2) witnesses.

The declarant voluntarily signed this document in my presence.

Witness #1 Signature _____

Printed Name _____

Address _____

Witness #2 Signature _____

Printed Name _____

Address _____

Nebraska Living Will Declaration

If I should lapse into a persistent vegetative state or have an incurable and irreversible condition that, without the administration of life-sustaining treatment, will, in the opinion of my attending physician, cause my death within a relatively short time and I am no longer able to make decisions regarding my medical treatment, then

I direct my attending physician, pursuant to the Rights of the Terminally Ill Act, to withhold or withdraw life sustaining treatment that is not necessary for my comfort or to alleviate pain.

Signed this _____ day of_____, 20_____.

Signature_____

Printed Name _____

Address _____

This document must either be witnessed by two (2) witnesses OR acknowledged before a Notary Public.

Witness Statements

The declarant voluntarily signed this writing in my presence.

Witness #1 Signature _____

Printed Name _____

Address _____

Witness #2 Signature _____

Printed Name _____

Address _____

Or

Notary Acknowledgement

The declarant voluntarily signed this writing in my presence.

_____
Notary Public

Nevada Living Will Declaration

If I should have an incurable and irreversible condition that, without the administration of life-sustaining treatment, will, in the opinion of my attending physician, cause my death within a relatively short time, and I am no longer able to make decisions regarding my medical treatment, then

I direct my attending physician, pursuant to NRS 449.535 to 449.690, inclusive, to withhold or withdraw treatment that only prolongs the process of dying and is not necessary for my comfort or to alleviate pain.

If you wish to include the following statement in this declaration, you must INITIAL the statement in the box provided:

[   ] Withholding or withdrawal of artificial nutrition and hydration may result in death by starvation or dehydration. Initial this box if you want to receive or continue receiving artificial nutrition and hydration by way of the gastro-intestinal tract after all other treatment is withheld pursuant to this declaration.

Signed this _____ day of_____, 20_____.

Signature _____

Printed Name _____

Address_____

This document must be witnesses by two (2) witnesses.

The declarant voluntarily signed this writing in my presence.

Witness #1 Signature _____

Printed Name _____

Address_____

Witness #2 Signature _____

Printed Name _____

Address_____

New Hampshire Living Will Declaration

Declaration made this ___ day of _____, 20___. I, _____, being of sound mind, willfully and voluntarily make known my desire that my dying shall not be artificially prolonged under the circumstances set forth below, do hereby declare:

If at any time I should have an incurable injury, disease, or illness certified to be a terminal condition or a permanently unconscious condition by two (2) physicians who have personally examined me, one of whom shall be my attending physician, and the physicians have determined that my death will occur whether or not life-sustaining procedures are utilized or that I will remain in a permanently unconscious condition and where the application of life-sustaining procedures would serve only to artificially prolong the dying process, I direct that such procedures be withheld or withdrawn, and that I be permitted to die naturally with only the administration of medication, sustenance, or the performance of any medical procedure deemed necessary to provide me with comfort care. I realize that situations could arise in which the only way to allow me to die would be to discontinue artificial nutrition and hydration.

In carrying out any instruction I have given under this section, I authorize that artificial nutrition and hydration not be started or, if started, be discontinued.

[yes]   [no]   Circle your choice and initial beneath it. If you do not choose "yes," artificial
[ ]   [ ]   nutrition and hydration will be provided and will not be removed.
  Initials

In the absence of my ability to give directions regarding the use of such life-sustaining procedures, it is my intention that this declaration shall be honored by my family and physicians as the final expression of my right to refuse medical or surgical treatment and accept the consequences of such refusal.

I understand the full import of this declaration, and I am emotionally and mentally competent to make this declaration.

Signed _____

We, the following witnesses, being duly sworn each declare to the notary public or justice of the peace or other official signing below (on reverse of form) as follows:
1. The declarant signed the instrument as a free and voluntary act for the purposes expressed, or expressly directed another to sign for him.
2. Each witness signed at the request of the declarant, in his presence, and in the presence of the other witness.
3. To the best of my knowledge, at the time of the signing the declarant was at least 18 years of age, and was of sane mind and under no constraint or undue influence.

Witness #1 Signature _____

Printed Name _____

Address _____

Witness #2 Signature _____

Printed Name _____

Address _____

State of _____

_____ County

The affidavit shall be made before a notary public or justice of the peace or other official authorized to administer oaths in the place of execution, who shall not also serve as a witness, and who shall complete and sign a certificate in content and form substantially as follows:

Sworn to and signed before me by _____, the declarant, and by the witnesses

_____ and _____, on _____.

_____

Signature

_____

Official Capacity

New Jersey Living Will Health Care Directive

If I am incapable of making an informed decision regarding my health care, I direct my loved ones and health care providers to follow my instructions as set forth below. (Initial all those that apply.)

(1) If I am diagnosed as having an incurable and irreversible illness, disease, or condition and if my attending physician and at least one additional physician who has personally examined me determine that my condition is terminal:

[   ] I direct that life-sustaining treatment which would serve only to artificially prolong my dying be withheld or ended. I also direct that I be given all medically appropriate treatment and care necessary to make me comfortable and to relieve pain.

[   ] I direct that life-sustaining treatment be continued, if medically appropriate.

(2) If there should come a time when I become permanently unconscious, and it is determined by my attending physician and at least one additional physician with appropriate expertise who has personally examined me, that I have totally and irreversibly lost consciousness and my ability to interact with other people and my surroundings:

[   ] I direct that life-sustaining treatment be withheld or discontinued. I understand that I will not experience pain or discomfort in this condition, and I direct that I be given all medically appropriate treatment and care necessary to provide for my personal hygiene and dignity.

[   ] I direct that life-sustaining treatment be continued, if medically appropriate.

(3) If there comes a time when I am diagnosed as having an incurable and irreversible illness, disease or condition which may not be terminal, but causes me to experience severe and worsening physical or mental deterioration, and I will never regain the ability to make decisions and express my wishes:

[   ] I direct that life-sustaining measures be withheld or discontinued and that I be given all medically appropriate care necessary to make me comfortable and to relieve pain.

[   ] I direct that life-sustaining treatment be continued, if medically appropriate.

(4) If I am receiving life-sustaining treatment that is experimental and not a proven therapy, or is likely to be ineffective or futile in prolonging life:

[   ] I direct that such life-sustaining treatment be withheld or withdrawn. I also direct that I be given all medically appropriate care necessary to make me comfortable and to relieve pain.

[   ] I direct that life-sustaining treatment be continued, if medically appropriate.

(5) If I am in the condition(s) described above I feel especially strongly about the following forms of treatment: (initial all those that apply)

[   ] I do not want cardiopulmonary resuscitation (CPR).

[   ] I do not want mechanical respiration.

[   ] I do not want tube feeding.

[   ] I do not want antibiotics.

[   ] I do want maximum pain relief, even if it may hasten my death.

(6) Pregnancy: If I am pregnant at the time that I am diagnosed as having any of the conditions described above, I direct that my health care provider comply with following instructions (optional):

(7) The State of New Jersey has determined that an individual may be declared legally dead when there has been an irreversible cessation of all functions of the entire brain, including the brain stem (also known as whole brain death). However, individuals who do not accept this definition of brain death because of their personal religious

beliefs may request that it not be applied in determining their death. Initial the following statement only if it applies to you:

[   ] To declare my death on the basis of the whole brain death standard would violate my personal religious beliefs. I therefore wish my death to be declared only when my heartbeat and breathing have irreversibly stopped.

Further Instructions:

By writing this advance directive, I inform those who may become responsible for my health care of my wishes and intend to ease the burdens of decision making which this responsibility may impose. I have discussed the terms of this designation with my health care representative(s) and my representative(s) has/have willingly agreed to accept the responsibility for acting on my behalf in accordance with this directive and my wishes. I understand the purpose and effect of this document and sign it knowingly, voluntarily and after careful deliberation.

Signed this _____ day of _____ 20 _____ .

Signature _____

Address _____

City _____ State _____

I declare that the person who signed this document or asked another to sign this document on his or her behalf, did so in my presence, that he or she is personally known to me and that he or she appears to be of sound mind and free of duress or undue influence. I am 18 years of age or older, and am not designated by this or any other document as the person's health care representative or alternate health care representative.

1. Witness Printed Name _____

Address _____

City _____ State _____

Signature _____ Date _____

2. Witness Printed Name _____

Address _____

City _____ State _____

Signature _____ Date _____

Or

On _____ , before me came _____ ,
          (date)   (name of declarant)
whom I know to be such person, and the declarant did then and there execute this declaration.

Sworn before me this _____ day of _____ , 20 _____ .

_____
Signature of Notary Public

New Mexico Living Will Instructions for Health Care

If you fill out this form, you may cross out any wording you do not want.

End-of-life Decisions: If I am unable to make or communicate decisions regarding my health care, and IF (i) I have an incurable or irreversible condition that will result in my death within a relatively short time, OR (ii) I become unconscious and, to a reasonable degree of medical certainty, I will not regain consciousness, OR (iii) the likely risks and burdens of treatment would outweigh the expected benefits, THEN I direct that my health-care providers and others involved in my care provide, withhold or withdraw treatment in accordance with the choice I have initialed below in one of the following three boxes:

[   ] I CHOOSE NOT To Prolong Life. I do not want my life to be prolonged.

[   ] I CHOOSE To Prolong Life. I want my life to be prolonged as long as possible within the limits of generally accepted health-care standards.

[   ] I CHOOSE To Let My Agent Decide. My agent under my power of attorney for health care may make life-sustaining treatment decisions for me.

Artificial Nutrition and Hydration: If I have chosen above NOT to prolong life, I also specify by marking my initials below:

[   ] I DO NOT want artificial nutrition OR

[   ] I DO want artificial nutrition.

[   ] I DO NOT want artificial hydration unless required for my comfort OR

[   ] I DO want artificial hydration.

Relief From Pain: Regardless of the choices I have made in this form and except as I state in the following space, I direct that the best medical care possible to keep me clean, comfortable and free of pain or discomfort be provided at all times so that my dignity is maintained, even if this care hastens my death:

Other Wishes: (If you wish to write your own instructions, or if you wish to add to the instructions you have given above, you may do so here.) I direct that: (Add additional sheets if needed.)

Effect of Copy: A copy of this form has the same effect as the original.

Revocation: I understand that I may revoke this ADVANCE HEALTH-CARE DIRECTIVE at any time, and that if I revoke it, I should promptly notify my supervising health-care provider and any health-care institution where I am receiving care and any others to whom I have given copies of this power of attorney. I understand that I may revoke the designation of an agent either by a signed writing or by personally informing the supervising health-care provider.

Signatures: Sign and date the form here. Optional witness signatures on reverse of form.

_____   _____
(date)   (sign your name)

_____   _____
(social security number)   (print your name)

_____
(address)

(Optional) Signatures of Witnesses:

First witness

_____
(print name)

_____
(address)

_____
(city)   (state)

_____
(signature of witness)

_____
(date)

Second witness

_____
(print name)

_____
(address)

_____
(city)   (state)

_____
(signature of witness)

_____
(date)

North Carolina Living Will Declaration of a Desire for a Natural Death

I, _____, being of sound mind, desire that, as specified below, my life not be prolonged by extraordinary means or by artificial nutrition or hydration if my condition is determined to be terminal and incurable or if I am diagnosed as being in a persistent vegetative state.

I am aware and understand that this writing authorizes a physician to withhold or discontinue extraordinary means or artificial nutrition or hydration, in accordance with my specifications set forth below:

(Initial any of the following, as desired):

[   ] If my condition is determined to be terminal and incurable, I authorize the following:
[   ] My physician may withhold or discontinue extraordinary means only.
[   ] In addition to withholding or discontinuing extraordinary means if such means are necessary, my
               physician may withhold or discontinue either artificial nutrition or hydration, or both.
[   ] If my physician determines that I am in a persistent vegetative state, I authorize the following:
[   ] My physician may withhold or discontinue extraordinary means only.

[   ] In addition to withholding or discontinuing extraordinary means if such means are necessary, my
               physician may withhold or discontinue either artificial nutrition or hydration, or both.

This the _____ day of _____, 20 ____.

Signature_____

I hereby state that the declarant,_____ , being of sound mind signed the above declaration in my presence and that I am not related to the declarant by blood or marriage and that I do not know or have a reasonable expectation that I would be entitled to any portion of the estate of the declarant under any existing will or codicil of the declarant or as an heir under the Intestate Succession Act if the declarant died on this date without a will. I also state that I am not the declarant's attending physician or an employee of the declarant's attending physician, or an employee of a health facility in which the declarant is a patient or an employee of a nursing home or any group-care home where the declarant resides. I further state that I do not now have any claim against the declarant.

Witness #1 Signature _____

Printed Name _____

Address _____

Witness #2 Signature _____

Printed Name _____

Address _____

The clerk or the assistant clerk, or a notary public may, upon proper proof, certify the declaration as follows on reverse of form:

Certificate

I, _____, Clerk (Assistant Clerk) of Superior Court or Notary Public (circle one as appropriate) for _____County hereby certify that_____, the declarant, appeared before me and swore to me and to the witnesses in my presence that this instrument is his Living Will Declaration of a Desire for a Natural Death, and that he had willingly and voluntarily made and executed it as his free act and deed for the purposes expressed in it.

I further certify that _____ and_____, witnesses, appeared before me and swore that they witnessed_____, declarant, sign the attached declaration, believing him to be of sound mind; and also swore that at the time they witnessed the declaration (i) they were not related within the third degree to the declarant or to the declarant's spouse, and (ii) they did not know or have a reasonable expectation that they would be entitled to any portion of the estate of the declarant upon the declarant's death under any will of the declarant or codicil thereto then existing or under the Intestate Succession Act as it provides at that time, and (iii) they were not a physician attending the declarant or an employee of an attending physician or an employee of a health facility in which the declarant was a patient or an employee of a nursing home or any group-care home in which the declarant resided, and (iv) they did not have a claim against the declarant. I further certify that I am satisfied as to the genuineness and due execution of the declaration.

This the _____ day of_____, 20____.

_____
Clerk (Assistant Clerk) of Superior Court or Notary Public (circle one as appropriate)
for the County of _____.

North Dakota Living Will Declaration

I, _____,
(name)

declare on _____ :
(month, day, year)

I have made the following decision concerning life-prolonging treatment:
(initial 1, 2, or 3)

[   ] 1. I direct that life-prolonging treatment be withheld or withdrawn and that I be permitted to die naturally if two physicians certify that: (a) I am in a terminal condition that is an incurable or irreversible condition which, without the administration of life-prolonging treatment, will result in my imminent death; (b) The application of life-prolonging treatment would serve only to artificially prolong the process of my dying; and (c) I am not pregnant. It is my intention that this declaration be honored by my family and physicians as the final expression of my legal right to refuse medical or surgical treatment and that they accept the consequences of that refusal, which is death.

[   ] 2. I direct that life-prolonging treatment, which could extend my life, be used if two physicians certify that I am in a terminal condition that is an incurable or irreversible condition which, without the administration of life-prolonging treatment, will result in my imminent death. It is my intention that this declaration be honored by my family and physicians as the final expression of my legal right to direct that medical or surgical treatment be provided.

[   ] 3. I make no statement concerning life-prolonging treatment.

I have made the following decision concerning the administration of nutrition when my death is imminent *(initial only one statement):*

[   ] (1) I wish to receive nutrition.

[   ] (2) I wish to receive nutrition unless I cannot physically assimilate nutrition, nutrition would be physically harmful or would cause unreasonable physical pain, or nutrition would only prolong the process of my dying.

[   ] (3) I do not wish to receive nutrition.

[   ] (4) I make no statement concerning the administration of nutrition.

I have made the following decision concerning the administration of hydration when my death is imminent *(initial only one statement):*

[   ] (1) I wish to receive hydration.

[   ] (2) I wish to receive nutrition unless I cannot physically assimilate nutrition, nutrition would be physically harmful or would cause unreasonable physical pain, or nutrition would only prolong the process of my dying.

[   ] (3) I do not wish to receive hydration.

[   ] (4) I make no statement concerning the administration of hydration.

Concerning the administration of nutrition and hydration, I understand that if I make no statement about nutrition or hydration, my attending physician may withhold or withdraw nutrition or hydration if the physician determines that I cannot physically assimilate nutrition or hydration or that nutrition or hydration would be physically harmful or would cause unreasonable physical pain.

If I have been diagnosed as pregnant and that diagnosis is known to my physician, this declaration is not effective during the course of my pregnancy.

Other Directions:

I understand the importance of this declaration, I am voluntarily signing this declaration, I am at least eighteen years of age, and I am emotionally and mentally competent to make this declaration.

I understand that I may revoke this declaration at any time.

Date And Signature of Principal

I sign my name to this Living Will Declaration on _____ (date)
at _____(city) _____ (state)

Your Signature _____

This living will not be valid unless it is notarized or signed by two qualified witnesses who are present when you sign or acknowledge your signature. If you have attached any additional pages to this form, you must date and sign each of the additional pages at the same time you date and sign this living will.

Option 1: Notary Public
In my presence on _____ (date), _____ (name of declarant) acknowledged the declarant's signature on this document or acknowledged that the declarant directed the person signing this document to sign on the declarant's behalf._____
(Signature of Notary Public)
My commission expires _____ , 20_____.

Option 2: Two Witnesses
Witness One:
(1) In my presence on _____ (date), _____ (name of declarant) acknowledged the declarant's signature on this document or acknowledged that the declarant directed the person signing this document to sign on the declarant's behalf. (2) I am at least eighteen years of age. (3) If I am a health care provider or an employee of a health care provider giving direct care to the declarant, I must initial this box: [   ]
I certify that the information in (1) through (3) is true and correct.

_____   _____
(Signature of Witness One)   (Printed Name of Witness One)

_____
(Address)

Witness Two:
(1) In my presence on_____ (date), _____ (name of declarant) acknowledged the declarant's signature on this document or acknowledged that the declarant directed the person signing this document to sign on the declarant's behalf. (2) I am at least eighteen years of age. (3) If I am a health care provider or an employee of a health care provider giving direct care to the declarant, I must initial this box: [   ]
I certify that the information in (1) through (3) is true and correct.

_____   _____
(Signature of Witness Two)   (Printed Name of Witness Two)

_____
(Address)

3. A physician or other health care provider who is furnished a copy of the declaration shall make it a part of the declarant's medical record and, if unwilling to comply with the declaration, promptly so advise the declarant.

Ohio Living Will Declaration

Notice to Declarant: This form of a Living Will Declaration is designed to serve as evidence of an individual's desire that life-sustaining medical treatment, including artificially or technologically supplied nutrition and hydration, be withheld or withdrawn if the individual is unable to communicate and is in a terminal condition or a permanently unconscious state. If you would choose not to withhold or withdraw any or all forms of life-sustaining treatment, you have the legal right to so choose and you might want to state your medical treatment preferences in writing in another form of Declaration. Under Ohio law a Living Will Declaration may be relied on only for individuals in a terminal condition or a permanently unconscious state. If you wish to direct your medical treatment in other circumstances, you should consider preparing a Durable Power of Attorney for Health Care.

I, _____, presently residing at _____(address), (the "Declarant"), being of sound mind and not subject to duress, fraud or undue influence, intending to create a Living Will Declaration under Chapter 2133 of the Ohio Revised Code, do voluntarily make known my desire that my dying shall not be artificially prolonged. If I am unable to give directions regarding the use of life-sustaining treatment when I am in a terminal condition or a permanently unconscious state, it is my intention that this Living Will Declaration shall be honored by my family and physicians as the final expression of my legal right to refuse medical or surgical treatment. I am a competent adult who understands and accepts the consequences of such refusal and the purpose and effect of this document. *(Initial all that you choose).*

In the event I am in a terminal condition, I declare and direct that my attending physician shall:

[   ] Administer no life-sustaining treatment, including cardiopulmonary resuscitation;

[   ] Withdraw life-sustaining treatment, including cardiopulmonary resuscitation, if such treatment has commenced and in the case of cardiopulmonary resuscitation issue a do-not-resuscitate order ; and,

[   ] Permit me to die naturally and provide me with only the care necessary to make me comfortable and to relieve my pain but not to postpone my death.

In the event I am in a permanently unconscious state, I declare and direct that my attending physician shall:

[   ] Administer no life-sustaining treatment, including cardiopulmonary resuscitation, except for the provision of artificially or technologically supplied nutrition or hydration unless, in the following paragraph, I have authorized its withholding or withdrawal;

[   ] Withdraw such treatment, including cardiopulmonary resuscitation, if such treatment has commenced; and, in the case of cardiopulmonary resuscitation issue a do-not-resuscitate order;

[   ] Permit me to die naturally and provide me with only that care necessary to make me comfortable and to relieve my pain but not to postpone my death.

[   ] In addition, if I have initialed the foregoing box, I authorize my attending physician to withhold, or in the event that treatment has already commenced, to withdraw the provision of artificially or technologically supplied nutrition and hydration, If I am in a permanently unconscious state and if my attending physician and at least one other physician who has examined me determine, to a reasonable degree of medical certainty and in accordance with reasonable medical standards, that such nutrition or hydration will not or no longer will serve to provide comfort to me or alleviate my pain.

In the event my attending physician determines that life-sustaining treatment should be withheld or withdrawn, he or she shall make a good faith effort and use reasonable diligence to notify one of the persons named below in the following order of priority:

1. _____(name) , _____(relationship)

presently residing at _____(address)

_____(phone and work phone numbers)

2. _____,(name) _____ (relationship)
presently residing at _____ (address)
_____ (phone and work phone numbers)

Any Other directions:

[   ] **I have a durable power of attorney for health care (initial if true).**

For purposes of this Living Will Declaration:
(A) "Life-sustaining treatment" means any medical procedure, treatment, intervention, or other measure including artificially or technologically supplied nutrition and hydration that, when administered, will serve principally to prolong the process of dying.
(B) "Terminal Condition" means an irreversible, incurable, and untreatable condition caused by disease, illness, or injury from which, to a reasonable degree of medical certainty as determined in accordance with reasonable medical standards by my attending physician and one other physician who has examined me, both of the following apply: (1) There can be no recovery; and (2) Death is likely to occur within a relatively short time if life-sustaining treatment is not administered.
(C) "Permanently Unconscious State" means a state of permanent unconsciousness that, to a reasonable degree of medical certainty as determined in accordance with reasonable medical standards by my attending physician and one other physician who has examined me, is characterized by both of the following: (1) I am irreversibly unaware of myself and my environment, and (2) There is a total loss of cerebral cortical functioning, resulting in my having no capacity to experience pain or suffering.

I understand the purpose and effect of this document and sign my name to this Living Will Declaration after careful deliberation on _____ (date), at _____ (city), Ohio.

Signature of Declarant _____

I attest that the Declarant signed or acknowledged this Living Will Declaration in my presence, and that the Declarant appears to be of sound mind and not under or subject to duress, fraud or undue influence. I further attest that I am not the attending physician of the Declarant, I am not the administrator of a nursing home in which the Declarant is receiving care, and that I am an adult not related to the Declarant by blood, marriage, or adoption.
Witness #1 Signature: _____
Print Name: _____
Residence Address: _____
Date: _____

Witness #2 Signature: _____
Print Name: _____
Residence Address: _____
Date: _____

Or

Acknowledgment

State of Ohio
County of _____
On this the _____ day of _____, 20 ____, before me, the undersigned Notary Public, personally appeared _____, known to me or satisfactorily proven to be the Declarant whose name is subscribed to the above Living Will Declaration, and acknowledged that (s)he executed the same for the purposes expressed therein. I attest that the Declarant appears to be of sound mind and not under or subject to duress, fraud or undue influence.
My Commission Expires:

_____ Signature of Notary Public

Oklahoma Living Will

I, _____, being of sound mind and eighteen (18) years of age or older, willfully and voluntarily make known my desire, by my instructions to others through my living will, or by my appointment of a health care proxy, or both, that my life shall not be artificially prolonged under the circumstances set forth below. I thus do hereby declare:

a. If my attending physician and another physician determine that I am no longer able to make decisions regarding my medical treatment, I direct my attending physician and other health care providers, pursuant to the Oklahoma Rights of the Terminally Ill or Persistently Unconscious Act, to withhold or withdraw treatment from me under the circumstances I have indicated below by my signature. I understand that I will be given treatment that is necessary for my comfort or to alleviate my pain.

b. **If I have a terminal condition**:
(1) I direct that life-sustaining treatment shall be withheld or withdrawn if such treatment would only prolong my process of dying, and if my attending physician and another physician determine that I have an incurable and irreversible condition that even with the administration of life-sustaining treatment will cause my death within six (6) months.
_____ (signature)

(2) I understand that the subject of the artificial administration of nutrition and hydration (food and water) that will only prolong the process of dying from an incurable and irreversible condition is of particular importance. I understand that if I do not sign this paragraph, artificially administered nutrition and hydration will be administered to me. I further understand that if I sign this paragraph, I am authorizing the withholding or withdrawal of artificially administered nutrition (food) and hydration (water).
_____ (signature)

(3) I direct that (add other medical directives, if any):

_____ (signature)

c. **If I am persistently unconscious**:
(1) I direct that life-sustaining treatment be withheld or withdrawn if such treatment will only serve to maintain me in an irreversible condition, as determined by my attending physician and another physician, in which thought and awareness of self and environment are absent.
_____ (signature)

(2) I understand that the subject of the artificial administration of nutrition and hydration (food and water) for individuals who have become persistently unconscious is of particular importance. I understand that if I do not sign this paragraph, artificially administered nutrition and hydration will be administered to me. I further understand that if I sign this paragraph, I am authorizing the withholding or withdrawal of artificially administered nutrition (food) and hydration (water).
_____ (signature)

(3) I direct that (add other medical directives, if any)

_____ (signature)

Signature and Witness Signatures on reverse side of form

Conflicting Provision

I understand that if I have completed both a living will and have appointed a health care proxy, and if there is a conflict between my health care proxy's decision and my living will, my living will shall take precedence unless I indicate otherwise.

_____ (signature)

General Provisions

a. I understand that if I have been diagnosed as pregnant and that diagnosis is known to my attending physician, This advance directive shall have no force or effect during the course of my pregnancy. b. In the absence of my ability to give directions regarding the use of life-sustaining procedures, it is my intention that this advance directive shall be honored by my family and physicians as the final expression of my legal right to refuse medical or surgical treatment including, but not limited to, the administration of any life-sustaining procedures, and I accept the consequences of such refusal. c. This advance directive shall be in effect until it is revoked. d. I understand that I may revoke this advance directive at any time. e. I understand and agree that if I have any prior directives, and if I sign this advance directive, my prior directives are revoked. f. I understand the full importance of this advance directive and I am emotionally and mentally competent to make this advance directive.

Signed this _____ day of _____, 20 _____ .

Signature of Declarant_____

  City, County and State of Residence_____

This advance directive was signed in my presence.

Witness #1 Signature _____

Printed Name _____

Address _____

Witness #2 Signature _____

Printed Name _____

Address _____

C. A physician or other health care provider who is furnished the original or a photocopy of the advance directive shall make it a part of the declarant's medical record and, if unwilling to comply with the advance directive, promptly so advise the declarant.

D. In the case of a qualified patient, the patient's health care proxy, in consultation with the attending physician, shall have the authority to make treatment decisions for the patient including the withholding or withdrawal of life-sustaining procedures if so indicated in the patient's advance directive.

E. A person executing an advanced directive appointing a health care proxy who may not have an attending physician for reasons based on established religious beliefs or tenets may designate an individual other than the designated health care proxy, in lieu of an attending physician and other physician, to determine the lack of decisional capacity of the person. Such designation shall be specified and included as part of the advanced directive executed pursuant to the provisions of this section.

Oregon Living Will Health Care Instructions

NOTE: This is an important legal document. It can control critical decisions about your health care. You have the right to give instructions for health care providers to follow if you become unable to direct your care. The term "as my physician recommends" means that you want your physician to try life support if your physician believes it could be helpful and then discontinue is if it is not helping your health condition or symptoms. Life support refers to any medical means for maintaining life, including procedures, devices and medications. If you refuse life support, you will still get routine measures to keep you clean and comfortable. Tube Feeding is one sort of life support where food and water are supplied artificially by medical device. If you refuse tube feeding, you should understand that malnutrition, dehydration and death will probably result. You will get care for your comfort and cleanliness, no matter what choices you make. You may either give specific instructions by filling out Items 1 to 4 below, or you may use the general instruction provided by Item 5. This form is valid only if you sign it voluntarily and when you are of sound mind. If you do not want a living will, you do not have to sign this form. You may revoke this document at any time. Despite this document, you have the right to decide your own health care as long as you are able to do so. If there is anything in this document that you do not understand, ask a lawyer to explain it to you. You may cross out words that don't express your wishes or add words that better express your wishes.

Here are my desires about my health care if my doctor and another knowledgeable doctor confirm that I am in a medical condition described below:

1. **Close to Death.** If I am close to death and life support would only postpone the moment of my death:
A. **Initial One:**
[   ] I want to receive tube feeding.
[   ] I want tube feeding only as my physician recommends.
[   ] I DO NOT WANT tube feeding.
B. **Initial One:**
[   ] I want any other life support that may apply.
[   ] I want life support only as my physician recommends.
[   ] I want NO life support.

2. **Permanently Unconscious.** If I am unconscious and it is very unlikely that I will ever become conscious again:
A. **Initial One:**
[   ] I want to receive tube feeding.
[   ] I want tube feeding only as my physician recommends.
[   ] I DO NOT WANT tube feeding.
B. **Initial One:**
[   ] I want any other life support that may apply.
[   ] I want life support only as my physician recommends.
[   ] I want NO life support.

3. **Advanced Progressive Illness.** If I have a progressive illness that will be fatal and is in an advanced stage, and I am consistently and permanently unable to communicate by any means, swallow food and water safely, care for myself and recognize my family and other people, and it is very unlikely that my condition will substantially improve:
A. **Initial One:**
[   ] I want to receive tube feeding.
[   ] I want tube feeding only as my physician recommends.
[   ] I DO NOT WANT tube feeding.

B. **Initial One:**

[   ] I want any other life support that may apply.

[   ] I want life support only as my physician recommends.

[   ] I want NO life support.

4. **Extraordinary Suffering.** If life support would not help my medical condition and would make me suffer permanent and severe pain:

A. **Initial One:**

[   ] I want to receive tube feeding.

[   ] I want tube feeding only as my physician recommends.

[   ] I DO NOT WANT tube feeding.

B. **Initial One:**

[   ] I want any other life support that may apply.

[   ] I want life support only as my physician recommends.

[   ] I want NO life support.

5. **General Instruction. Initial if this applies:**

[   ] I do not want my life to be prolonged by life support. I also do not want tube feeding as life support. I want my doctors to allow me to die naturally if my doctor and another knowledgeable doctor confirm I am in any of the medical conditions listed in Items 1 to 4 above.

6. **Additional Conditions or Instructions.** (Insert description of what you want done.) :

7. **Other Documents.** A health care power of attorney is any document you may have signed to appoint a representative to make health care decisions for you. **Initial One:**

[   ] I have previously signed a health care power of attorney. I want it to remain in effect unless I appointed a health care representative after signing the health care
power of attorney.

[   ] I have a health care power of attorney, and I REVOKE IT.

[   ] I DO NOT have a health care power of attorney.

Date _____ Printed Name of Declarant _____ Birth Date _____

Signature of Declarant _____

Declaration of Witnesses

We declare that the person signing this advance directive:

(a) Is personally known to us or has provided proof of identity;

(b) Signed or acknowledged that person's signature on this advance directive in our presence;

(c) Appears to be of sound mind and not under duress, fraud or undue influence;

(d) Has not appointed either of us as health care representative or alternative representative; and

(e) Is not a patient for whom either of us is attending physician.

_____

Signature of Witness   Printed name   date

_____

Signature of Witness   Printed name   date

NOTE: One witness must not be a relative (by blood, marriage or adoption) of the person signing this advance directive. That witness must also not be entitled to any portion of the person's estate upon death. That witness must also not own, operate or be employed at a health care facility where the person is a patient or resident.

Pennsylvania Living Will Declaration

I,_____, being of sound mind, willfully and voluntarily make this declaration to be followed if I become incompetent. This declaration reflects my firm and settled commitment to refuse life-sustaining treatment under the circumstances indicated below.

I direct my attending physician to withhold or withdraw life-sustaining treatment that serves only to prolong the process of my dying, if I should be in a terminal condition or in a state of permanent unconsciousness.

I direct that treatment be limited to measures to keep me comfortable and to relieve pain, including any pain that might occur by withholding or withdrawing life-sustaining treatment.

In addition, if I am in the condition described above, I feel especially strong about the following forms of treatment:

I [   ] do   or [   ] do not want cardiac resuscitation.
I [   ] do   or [   ] do not want mechanical respiration.
I [   ] do   or [   ] do not want tube feeding or any other artificial or invasive form of
                          nutrition (food) or hydration (water).
I [   ] do   or [   ] do not want blood or blood products.
I [   ] do   or [   ] do not want any form of surgery or invasive diagnostic tests.
I [   ] do   or [   ] do not want kidney dialysis.
I [   ] do   or [   ] do not want antibiotics.

I realize that if I do not specifically indicate my preference regarding any of the forms of treatment listed above, I may receive that form of treatment.

Other instructions:

I made this declaration on the _____ day of _____ 20___.

_____
Declarant's signature

_____
Declarant's address

The declarant or the person on behalf of and at the direction of declarant knowingly and voluntarily signed this writing by signature or mark in my presence.

Witness #1 signature:_____ Printed name _____

Witness's address:_____

Witness #2 signature:_____ Printed name _____

Witness's address:_____

Rhode Island Living Will Declaration

I, _____, being of sound mind willfully and voluntarily make known my desire that my dying shall not be artificially prolonged under the circumstances set forth below, do hereby declare:

If I should have an incurable or irreversible condition that without the administration of life-sustaining procedures will cause my death, and if I am unable to make decisions regarding my medical treatment, then

I direct my attending physician to withhold or withdraw procedures that merely prolong the dying process and are not necessary to my comfort, or to alleviate pain.

Other directions:

This authorization:

[   ] includes **or** [   ] does not include

the withholding or withdrawal of artificial feeding (check only one box above).

Signed this_____ day of _____, 20_____.

Signature_____

Address_____

The declarant is personally known to me and voluntarily signed this document in my presence.

Witness #1 Signature _____

Printed Name _____

Address _____

Witness #2 Signature _____

Printed Name _____

Address _____

South Carolina Living Will Declaration of a Desire for a Natural Death

I, _____, Declarant, being at least eighteen years of age and a resident of and domiciled in the City of _____, County of _____, State of South Carolina, make this Declaration this ____ day of _____, 20___.

I willfully and voluntarily make known my desire that no life-sustaining procedures be used to prolong my dying if my condition is terminal or if I am in a state of permanent unconsciousness, and I declare:

If at any time I have a condition certified to be a terminal condition by two physicians who have personally examined me, one of whom is my attending physician, and the physicians have determined that my death could occur within a reasonably short period of time without the use of life-sustaining procedures or if the physicians certify that I am in a state of permanent unconsciousness and where the application of life-sustaining procedures would serve only to prolong the dying process, I direct that the procedures be withheld or withdrawn, and that I be permitted to die naturally with only the administration of medication or the performance of any medical procedure necessary to provide me with comfort care.

Instructions Concerning Artificial Nutrition And Hydration
Initial One of The Following Statements:
If my condition is terminal and could result in death within a reasonably short time,
[   ] I direct that nutrition and hydration BE PROVIDED through any medically indicated means, including medically or surgically implanted tubes.
[   ] I direct that nutrition and hydration NOT BE PROVIDED through any medically indicated means, including medically or surgically implanted tubes.

Initial One of the Following Statements:
If I am in a persistent vegetative state or other condition of permanent unconsciousness,
[   ] I direct that nutrition and hydration BE PROVIDED through any medically indicated means, including medically or surgically implanted tubes.
[   ] I direct that nutrition and hydration NOT BE PROVIDED through any medically indicated means, including medically or surgically implanted tubes.

In the absence of my ability to give directions regarding the use of life-sustaining procedures, it is my intention that this Declaration be honored by my family and physicians and any health facility in which I may be a patient as the final expression of my legal right to refuse medical or surgical treatment, and I accept the consequences from the refusal. I am aware that this Declaration authorizes a physician to withhold or withdraw life-sustaining procedures. I am emotionally and mentally competent to make this Declaration.

_____
Signature of Declarant

Affidavit

State of South Carolina
County of _____
We, _____ and _____, the undersigned witnesses to the foregoing Declaration, dated the ____ day of _____, 20___, at least one of us being first duly sworn, declare to the undersigned authority, on the basis of our best information and belief, that the Declaration was on that date signed by the declarant as and for his Living Will Declaration of a Desire for a Natural Death in our presence and we, at his request and in his presence, and in the presence of each other, subscribe our names as

witnesses on that date. The declarant is personally known to us, and we believe him to be of sound mind. Each of us affirms that he is qualified as a witness to this Declaration under the provisions of the South Carolina Death With Dignity Act in that he is not related to the declarant by blood, marriage, or adoption, either as a spouse, lineal ancestor, descendant of the parents of the declarant, or spouse of any of them; nor directly financially responsible for the declarant's medical care; nor entitled to any portion of the declarant's estate upon his decease, whether under any will or as an heir by intestate succession; nor the beneficiary of a life insurance policy of the declarant; nor the declarant's attending physician; nor an employee of the attending physician; nor a person who has a claim against the declarant's decedent's estate as of this time. No more than one of us is an employee of a health facility in which the declarant is a patient. If the declarant is a resident in a hospital or nursing care facility at the date of execution of this Declaration, at least one of us is an ombudsman designated by the State Ombudsman, Office of the Governor.

Witness #1 Signature _____

Printed Name _____

Address _____

Witness #2 Signature _____

Printed Name _____

Address _____

Subscribed before me by _____, the declarant, and subscribed and sworn to before me by _____, the witnesses, this _____ day of _____, 20___.

_____
Signature

Notary Public for _____

My commission expires: _____

South Dakota Living Will Declaration

This is an important legal document. This document directs the medical treatment you are to receive in the event you are unable to participate in your own medical decisions and you are in a terminal condition. This document may state what kind of treatment you want or do not want to receive. This document can control whether you live or die. Prepare this document carefully. If you use this form, read it completely. You may want to seek professional help to make sure the form does what you intend and is completed without mistakes. This document will remain valid and in effect until and unless you revoke it. Review this document periodically to make sure it continues to reflect your wishes. You may amend or revoke this document at any time by notifying your physician and other health-care providers. You should give copies of this document to your physician and your family. This form is entirely optional. *If you choose to use this form, please note that the form provides signature lines for you, the two witnesses whom you have selected and a notary public.*

To My Family, Physicians, and All Those Concerned with My Care:

I, _____, willfully and voluntarily make this declaration as a directive to be followed if I am in a terminal condition and become unable to participate in decisions regarding my medical care. With respect to any life-sustaining treatment, I direct the following: (Initial only one of the following optional directives if you agree. If you do not agree with any of the following directives, space is provided below for you to write your own directives).

[ ] **No Life-sustaining Treatment.** I direct that no life-sustaining treatment be provided. If life-sustaining treatment is begun, terminate it.

[ ] **Treatment For Restoration.** Provide life-sustaining treatment only if and for so long as you believe treatment offers a reasonable possibility of restoring to me the ability to think and act for myself.

[ ] **Treat Unless Permanently Unconscious.** If you believe that I am permanently unconscious and are satisfied that this condition is irreversible, then do not provide me with life-sustaining treatment, and if life-sustaining treatment is being provided to me, terminate it. If and so long as you believe that treatment has a reasonable possibility of restoring consciousness to me, then provide life-sustaining treatment.

[ ] **Maximum Treatment.** Preserve my life as long as possible, but do not provide treatment that is not in accordance with accepted medical standards as then in effect. (Artificial nutrition and hydration is food and water provided by means of a nasogastric tube or tubes inserted into the stomach, intestines, or veins. If you do not wish to receive this form of treatment, you must initial the statement below which reads: "I intend to include this treatment, among the 'life-sustaining treatment' that may be withheld or withdrawn.")

With respect to artificial nutrition and hydration, I wish to make clear that (Initial only one)

[ ] I intend to include this treatment among the "life-sustaining treatment" that may be withheld or withdrawn.

[ ] I do not intend to include this treatment among the "life-sustaining treatment" that may be withheld or withdrawn.

(If you do not agree with any of the printed directives and want to write your own, or if you want to write directives in addition to the printed provisions, or if you want to express some of your other thoughts, you can do so here):

Date: _____   Signature _____

Printed Name_____

Address _____

The declarant voluntarily signed this document in my presence.

Witness #1 Signature _____

Printed Name _____

Address _____

Witness #2 Signature _____

Printed Name _____

Address _____

Notary Acknowledgement

On this the _____ day of _____, 20_____, the declarant, _____,
and witnesses _____, and _____ personally
appeared before the undersigned officer and signed the foregoing instrument in my presence.

_____
Notary Public

My commission expires: _____.

Tennessee Living Will

I, _____, willfully and voluntarily make known my desire that my dying shall not be artificially prolonged under the circumstances set forth below, and do hereby declare:

If at any time I should have a terminal condition and my attending physician has determined there is no reasonable medical expectation of recovery and which, as a medical probability, will result in my death, regardless of the use or discontinuance of medical treatment implemented for the purpose of sustaining life, or the life process, I direct that medical care be withheld or withdrawn, and that I be permitted to die naturally with only the administration of medications or the performance of any medical procedure deemed necessary to provide me with comfortable care or to alleviate pain.

Artificially Provided Nourishment and Fluids:
By checking the appropriate line below, I specifically:

[   ] Authorize the withholding or withdrawal of artificially provided food, water or other nourishment or fluids.

[   ] DO NOT authorize the withholding or withdrawal of artificially provided food, water or other nourishment or fluids.

In the absence of my ability to give directions regarding my medical care, it is my intention that this declaration shall be honored by my family and physician as the final expression of my legal right to refuse medical care and accept the consequences of such refusal. The definitions of terms used herein shall be as set forth in the Tennessee Right to Natural Death Act, Tennessee Code Annotated, § 32-11-103. I understand the full import of this declaration, and I am emotionally and mentally competent to make this declaration.

In acknowledgment whereof, I do hereinafter affix my signature on this the _____ day of _____, 20____.

_____
Declarant Signature

This document must be witnessed by two (2) witnesses and acknowledged before a Notary Public.

We, the subscribing witnesses hereto, are personally acquainted with and subscribe our names hereto at the request of the declarant, an adult, whom we believe to be of sound mind, fully aware of the action taken herein and its possible consequence. We, the undersigned witnesses, further declare that we are not related to the declarant by blood or marriage; that we are not entitled to any portion of the estate of the declarant upon the declarant's decease under any will or codicil thereto presently existing or by operation of law then existing; that we are not the attending physician, an employee of the attending physician or a health facility in which the declarant is a patient; and that we are not persons who, at the present time, have a claim against any portion of the estate of the declarant upon the declarant's death.

_____   _____
Witness #1 Signature   Printed Name of Witness #1

_____   _____
Witness #2 Signature   Printed Name of Witness #2

Notary Public Acknowledgement on reverse of form.

State of Tennessee

County of _____

Subscribed, sworn to and acknowledged before me by _____, the declarant, and subscribed and sworn to before me by _____ and _____, witnesses, this _____ day of _____, 20____.

_____
Notary Public

My Commission Expires:_____

Texas Directive to Physicians and Family or Surrogates

Instructions for completing this document: This is an important legal document known as an Advance Directive. It is designed to help you communicate your wishes about medical treatment at some time in the future when you are unable to make your wishes known because of illness or injury. These wishes are usually based on personal values. In particular, you may want to consider what burdens or hardships of treatment you would be willing to accept for a particular amount of benefit obtained if you were seriously ill. You are encouraged to discuss your values and wishes with your family or chosen spokesperson, as well as your physician. Your physician, other health care provider, or medical institution may provide you with various resources to assist you in completing your advance directive. Brief definitions are listed below and may aid you in your discussions and advance planning. Initial the treatment choices that best reflect your personal preferences. Provide a copy of your directive to your physician, usual hospital, and family or spokesperson. Consider a periodic review of this document. By periodic review, you can best assure that the directive reflects your preferences. In addition to this advance directive, Texas law provides for two other types of directives that can be important during a serious illness. These are the Medical Power of Attorney and the Out-of-Hospital Do-Not-Resuscitate Order. You may wish to discuss these with your physician, family, hospital representative, or other advisers. You may also wish to complete a directive related to the donation of organs and tissues.

I, _____, recognize that the best health care is based upon a partnership of trust and communication with my physician. My physician and I will make health care decisions together as long as I am of sound mind and able to make my wishes known. If there comes a time that I am unable to make medical decisions about myself because of illness or injury, I direct that the following treatment preferences be honored:

If, in the judgment of my physician, I am suffering with a terminal condition from which I am expected to die within six months, even with available life-sustaining treatment provided in accordance with prevailing standards of medical care: (initial one)

[   ] I request that all treatments other than those needed to keep me comfortable be discontinued or withheld and my physician allow me to die as gently as possible; **OR**

[   ] I request that I be kept alive in this terminal condition using available life-sustaining treatment. (**This Selection Does Not Apply to Hospice Care**.)

If, in the judgment of my physician, I am suffering with an irreversible condition so that I cannot care for myself or make decisions for myself and am expected to die without life-sustaining treatment provided in accordance with prevailing standards of care: (initial one)

[   ] I request that all treatments other than those needed to keep me comfortable be discontinued or withheld and my physician allow me to die as gently as possible; **OR**

[   ] I request that I be kept alive in this irreversible condition using available life-sustaining treatment. (**This Selection Does Not Apply to Hospice Care**.)

Additional requests: (After discussion with your physician, you may wish to consider listing particular treatments in this space that you do or do not want in specific circumstances, such as artificial nutrition and fluids, intravenous antibiotics, etc. Be sure to state whether you do or do not want the particular treatment.)

After signing this directive, if my representative or I elect hospice care, I understand and agree that only those treatments needed to keep me comfortable would be provided and I would not be given available life-sustaining treatments.

If I do not have a Medical Power of Attorney, and I am unable to make my wishes known, I designate the following person(s) to make treatment decisions with my physician compatible with my personal values:

1._____

2._____

(If a Medical Power of Attorney has been executed, then an agent already has been named and you should not list additional names in this document.)

If the above persons are not available, or if I have not designated a spokesperson, I understand that a spokesperson will be chosen for me following standards specified in the laws of Texas. If, in the judgment of my physician, my death is imminent within minutes to hours, even with the use of all available medical treatment provided within the prevailing standard of care, I acknowledge that all treatments may be withheld or removed except those needed to maintain my comfort. I understand that under Texas law this directive has no effect if I have been diagnosed as pregnant. This directive will remain in effect until I revoke it. No other person may do so.

Signed_____ Date_____

City, County, State of Residence _____

Two competent adult witnesses must sign below, acknowledging the signature of the declarant. The witness designated as Witness 1 may not be a person designated to make a treatment decision for the patient and may not be related to the patient by blood or marriage. This witness may not be entitled to any part of the estate and may not have a claim against the estate of the patient. This witness may not be the attending physician or an employee of the attending physician. If this witness is an employee of a health care facility in which the patient is being cared for, this witness may not be involved in providing direct patient care to the patient. This witness may not be an officer, director, partner, or business office employee of a health care facility in which the patient is being cared for or of any parent organization of the health care facility.

Witness #1 Signature _____

Printed Name _____

Address _____

Witness #2 Signature _____

Printed Name _____

Address _____

Utah Directive to Physicians and Providers of Medical Services
(Pursuant to Section 75-2-1104, UCA)

This directive is made this _____ (date)

1. I , _____, (name)
being of sound mind, willfully and voluntarily make known my desire that my life not be artificially prolonged by life-sustaining procedures except as I may otherwise provide in this directive.

2. I declare that if at any time I should have an injury, disease, or illness, which is certified in writing to be a terminal condition or persistent vegetative state by two physicians who have personally examined me, and in the opinion of those physicians the application of life-sustaining procedures would serve only to unnaturally prolong the moment of my death and to unnaturally postpone or prolong the dying process, I direct that these procedures be withheld or withdrawn and my death be permitted to occur naturally.

3. I expressly intend this directive to be a final expression of my legal right to refuse medical or surgical treatment and to accept the consequences from this refusal which shall remain in effect notwithstanding my future inability to give current medical directions to treating physicians and other providers of medical services.

4. I understand that the term "life-sustaining procedure" includes artificial nutrition and hydration and any other procedures that I specify below to be considered life-sustaining but does not include the administration of medication or the performance of any medical procedure which is intended to provide comfort care or to alleviate pain.

Other Instructions: (optional)

5. I reserve the right to give current medical directions to physicians and other providers of medical services so long as I am able, even though these directions may conflict with the above written directive that life-sustaining procedures be withheld or withdrawn.

6. I understand the full import of this directive and declare that I am emotionally and mentally competent to make this directive.

_____
(declarant's signature)

_____
(city, county, and state of residence)

This document must be witnessed by two (2) witnesses. Witness signature spaces are on reverse side of form.

We witnesses certify that each of us is 18 years of age or older and each personally witnessed the declarant sign or direct the signing of this directive; that we are acquainted with the declarant and believe him or her to be of sound mind; that the declarant's desires are as expressed above; that neither of us is a person who signed the above directive on behalf of the declarant; that we are not related to the declarant by blood or marriage nor are we entitled to any portion of declarant's estate according to the laws of intestate succession of this state or under any will or codicil of declarant; that we are not directly financially responsible for declarant's medical care; and that we are not agents of any health care facility in which the declarant may be a patient at the time of signing this directive.

Witness #1 Signature _____

Printed Name _____

Address _____

Witness #2 Signature _____

Printed Name _____

Address _____

Vermont Living Will Terminal Care Document

To my family, my physician, my lawyer, my clergyman. To any medical facility in whose care I happen to be. To any individual who may become responsible for my health, welfare or affairs.

Death is as much a reality as birth, growth, maturity and old age-it is the one certainty of life. If the time comes when I, _____, can no longer take part in decisions of my own future, let this statement stand as an expression of my wishes, while I am still of sound mind.

If the situation should arise in which I am in a terminal state and there is no reasonable expectation of my recovery, I direct that I be allowed to die a natural death and that my life not be prolonged by extraordinary measures. I do, however, ask that medication be mercifully administered to me to alleviate suffering even though this may shorten my remaining life.

This statement is made after careful consideration and is in accordance with my strong convictions and beliefs. I want the wishes and directions here expressed carried out to the extent permitted by law. Insofar as they are not legally enforceable, I hope that those to whom this will is addressed will regard themselves as morally bound by these provisions.

Signed: _____

Date: _____

This Document must be witnessed by two (2) witnesses.

Witness #1 Signature _____

Printed Name _____

Address _____

Witness #2 Signature _____

Printed Name _____

Address _____

Copies of this request have been given to:

_____

_____

_____

Virginia Living Will Advance Medical Directive

I,_____, willfully and voluntarily make known my desire and do hereby declare:
If at any time my attending physician should determine that I have a terminal condition where the application of life-prolonging procedures would serve only to artificially prolong the dying process, then

I direct that such procedures be withheld or withdrawn, and that I be permitted to die naturally with only the administration of medication or the performance of any medical procedure deemed necessary to provide me with comfort care or to alleviate pain.

Other directions: I specifically direct that the following procedures or treatments be provided to me:

In the absence of my ability to give directions regarding the use of such life-prolonging procedures, it is my intention that this advance directive shall be honored by my family and physician as the final expression of my legal right to refuse medical or surgical treatment and accept the consequences of such refusal.

This advance directive shall not terminate in the event of my disability.

By signing below, I indicate that I am emotionally and mentally competent to make this advance directive and that I understand the purpose and effect of this document.

_____   _____
(Date)   (Signature of Declarant)

The declarant signed the foregoing advance directive in my presence. I am not the spouse or a blood relative of the declarant.

Witness #1 Signature _____

Printed Name _____

Address _____

Witness #2 Signature _____

Printed Name _____

Address _____

Washington Living Will Health Care Directive

Directive made this _____ day of_____, 20____.

I_____, having the capacity to make health care decisions, willfully, and voluntarily make known my desire that my dying shall not be artificially prolonged under the circumstances set forth below, and do hereby declare that:

(a) If at any time I should be diagnosed in writing to be in a terminal condition by the attending physician, or in a permanent unconscious condition by two physicians, and where the application of life-sustaining treatment would serve only to artificially prolong the process of my dying, I direct that such treatment be withheld or withdrawn, and that I be permitted to die naturally. I understand by using this form that a terminal condition means an incurable and irreversible condition caused by injury, disease, or illness, that would within reasonable medical judgment cause death within a reasonable period of time in accordance with accepted medical standards, and where the application of life-sustaining treatment would serve only to prolong the process of dying. I further understand in using this form that a permanent unconscious condition means an incurable and irreversible condition in which I am medically assessed within reasonable medical judgment as having no reasonable probability of recovery from an irreversible coma or a persistent vegetative state.

(b) In the absence of my ability to give directions regarding the use of such life-sustaining treatment, it is my intention that this directive shall be honored by my family and physician(s) as the final expression of my legal right to refuse medical or surgical treatment and I accept the consequences of such refusal. If another person is appointed to make these decisions for me, whether through a durable power of attorney or otherwise, I request that the person be guided by this directive and any other clear expressions of my desires.

(c) If I am diagnosed to be in a terminal condition or in a permanent unconscious condition (check one):
[   ] I DO want to have artificially provided nutrition and hydration.
[   ] I DO NOT want to have artificially provided nutrition and hydration.

(d) If I have been diagnosed as pregnant and that diagnosis is known to my physician, this directive shall have no force or effect during the course of my pregnancy.

(e) I understand the full import of this directive and I am emotionally and mentally capable to make the health care decisions contained in this directive.

(f) I understand that before I sign this directive, I can add to or delete from or otherwise change the wording of this directive and that I may add to or delete from this directive at any time and that any changes shall be consistent with Washington state law or federal constitutional law to be legally valid.

(g) It is my wish that every part of this directive be fully implemented. If for any reason any part is held invalid it is my wish that the remainder of my directive be implemented.

Signed_____

City, County, and State of Residence _____

The declarer has been personally known to me and I believe him or her to be capable of making health care decisions.

Witness #1 Signature _____   Printed Name _____

Address _____

Witness #2 Signature _____   Printed Name _____

Address _____

West Virginia Living Will

The Kind of Medical Treatment I Want and Don't Want If I Have
A Terminal Condition or Am In a Persistent Vegetative State

Living will made this_____ day of _____, 20_____. I,_____,
being of sound mind, willfully and voluntarily declare that I want my wishes to be respected if I am very sick and
not able to communicate my wishes for myself. In the absence of my ability to give directions regarding the use
of life-prolonging medical intervention, it is my desire that my dying shall not be prolonged under the following
circumstances:

If I am very sick and not able to communicate my wishes for myself and I am certified by one physician who has
personally examined me, to have a terminal condition or to be in a persistent vegetative state (I am unconscious
and am neither aware of my environment nor able to interact with others,) I direct that life-prolonging medical
intervention that would serve solely to prolong the dying process or maintain me in a persistent vegetative state
be withheld or withdrawn. I want to be allowed to die naturally and only be given medications or other medical
procedures necessary to keep me comfortable. I want to receive as much medication as is necessary to alleviate
my pain.

I Give the Following Special Directives or Limitations: (Comments about tube feedings, breathing machines,
cardiopulmonary resuscitation, dialysis and mental health treatment may be placed here. My failure to provide
special directives or limitations does not mean that I want or refuse certain treatments.):

It is my intention that this living will be honored as the final expression of my legal right to refuse medical or
surgical treatment and accept the consequences resulting from such refusal. I understand the full import of this
living will.

Signed_____

Address_____

I did not sign the principal's signature above for or at the direction of the principal. I am at least eighteen years of
age and am not related to the principal by blood or marriage, entitled to any portion of the estate of the principal
to the best of my knowledge under any will of principal or codicil thereto, or directly financially responsible for
principal's medical care. I am not the principal's attending physician or the principal's medical power of attorney
representative or successor medical power of attorney representative under a medical power of attorney.

Witness #1 Signature _____Date_____

Printed name of Witness #1 _____

Witness #2 Signature _____Date_____

Printed name of Witness #1 _____

Notary Acknowledgement on reverse side

STATE OF WEST VIRGINIA
COUNTY OF_____

I,_____ , a Notary Public of said County, do certify that _____ ,
as principal, and _____ , and _____ as witnesses,
whose names are signed to the writing above bearing date on the_____ day of ,_____ 20___ , have
this day acknowledged the same before me.

Given under my hand this day of_____ , 20_____ .
My commission expires:_____

_____
Signature of Notary Public

Wisconsin Living Will Declaration to Physicians

I,_____, being of sound mind, voluntarily state my desire that my dying not be prolonged under the circumstances specified in this document. Under those circumstances, I direct that I be permitted to die naturally. If I am unable to give directions regarding the use of life-sustaining procedures or feeding tubes, I intend that my family and physician honor this document as the final expression of my legal right to refuse medical or surgical treatment

1. **If I Have a Terminal Condition**, as determined by 2 physicians who have personally examined me, I do not want my dying to be artificially prolonged and I do not want life-sustaining procedures to be used. In Addition, the Following Are My Directions Regarding the Use of Feeding Tubes: **(Initial one)**
[   ]YES, I want feeding tubes used if I have a terminal condition.
[   ] NO, I do not want feeding tubes used if I have a terminal condition.
If you have not initialed either box, feeding tubes will be used.

2. **If I Am in a Persistent Vegetative State**, as determined by 2 physicians who have personally examined me, the following are my directions regarding the use of life-sustaining Procedures: **(Initial One)**
[   ] YES, I want life-sustaining procedures used if I am in a persistent vegetative state.
[   ] NO, I do not want life-sustaining procedures used if I am in a persistent vegetative state.
If you have not initialed either box, life-sustaining procedures will be used.

3. **If I Am in a Persistent Vegetative State**, as determined by 2 physicians who have personally examined me, the following are my directions regarding the use of feeding Tubes: **(Initial One)**
[   ] YES, I want feeding tubes used if I am in a persistent vegetative state.
[   ] NO, I do not want feeding tubes used if I am in a persistent vegetative state.
If you have not initialed either box, feeding tubes will be used.

Attention: You and the 2 witnesses must sign the document at the same time.

Signed _____Date_____

Address _____Date of birth_____

I believe that the person signing this document is of sound mind. I am an adult and am not related to the person signing this document by blood, marriage or adoption. I am not entitled to and do not have a claim on any portion of the person's estate and am not otherwise restricted by law from being a witness

Witness signature _____Date _____

Print name_____

Address _____

Witness signature _____Date _____

Print name_____

Address _____

Wyoming Living Will Declaration

Declaration made this _____ day of _____ 20___. I,_____, being of sound mind, willfully and voluntarily make known my desire that my dying shall not be artificially prolonged under the circumstances set forth below, do hereby declare:

If at any time I should have an incurable injury, disease or other illness certified to be a terminal condition by two (2) physicians who have personally examined me, one (1) of whom shall be my attending physician, and the physicians have determined that my death will occur whether or not life-sustaining procedures are utilized and where the application of life-sustaining procedures would serve only to artificially prolong the dying process, I direct that such procedures be withheld or withdrawn, and that I be permitted to die naturally with only the administration of medication or the performance of any medical procedure deemed necessary to provide me with comfort care.

If, in spite of this declaration, I am comatose or otherwise unable to make treatment decisions for myself, I HEREBY designate_____ to make treatment decisions for me.

In the absence of my ability to give directions regarding the use of life-sustaining procedures, it is my intention that this declaration shall be honored by my family and physician(s) and agent as the final expression of my legal right to refuse medical or surgical treatment and accept the consequences from this refusal. I understand the full import of this declaration and I am emotionally and mentally competent to make this declaration.

Signed_____

City, County and State of Residence _____

The declarant has been personally known to me and I believe him or her to be of sound mind. I did not sign the declarant's signature above for or at the direction of the declarant. I am not related to the declarant by blood or marriage, entitled to any portion of the estate of the declarant according to the laws of intestate succession or under any will of the declarant or codicil thereto, or directly financially responsible for declarant's medical care.

Witness #1 Signature _____

Printed Name _____

Address _____

Witness #2 Signature _____

Printed Name _____

Address _____

NOTICE: This document has significant medical, legal and possible ethical implications and effects. Before you sign this document, you should become completely familiar with these implications and effects. The operation, effects and implications of this document may be discussed with a physician, a lawyer and a clergyman of your choice.